Advanced Drumming Coordination

A Comprehensive Guide to Four-Way Independence

Ray Rojo

Violet Anamnesis Publications

SAN DIEGO, CALIFORNIA

Copyright © 2019 by Violet Anamnesis Publications

All rights reserved. No part of this publication may be reproduced, distributed or transmitted in any form or by any means, including photocopying, recording, or other electronic or mechanical methods, without prior written permission from the publisher, except in the case of brief quotations embodied in critical reviews and certain other noncommercial uses permitted by copyright law. For permission requests, write to the publisher, addressed "Attention: Permissions Coordinator," at the address below.

Violet Anamnesis Publications
11880 Bernardo Terrace Suite B
San Diego, CA/ 92128
www.violetanamnesispublications.com

Cover artwork by Luis Chiwo López

Advanced Drumming Coordination/Ray Rojo -- 1st ed.
ISBN 978-1-944213-42-8

In memory of Travis Cuauhtémoc Martínez Suárez

Table of Contents

Acknowledgments iii

Foreword by Sebastian Lanser v

Introduction vi

Audio Download viii

Chapter 1: Same Pattern, Same Note Value 1

    1.A.- Concept Introduction - Single Stroke Roll 2

    1.B.- Concept Development Part 1 - Double Stroke Roll 5

    1.C.- Concept Development Part 2 - Paradiddle 7

    1.D.- Suggested Patterns 9

Chapter 2: Coordinating One Voice Over Two-Limb Ostinatos 12

    2.A.- Concept Introduction - Groups of Three as an Ostinato 13

    2.B.- Concept Development Part 1 - Rhythmic Ideas Over the Ostinato 23

    2.C.- Concept Development Part 2 - Modifying the Ostinato 27

Chapter 3: Same Pattern, Different Note Value – Same Ratio 30

    3.A.- Concept Introduction - Single Stroke Roll 31

    3.B.- Concept Development Part 1 - Double Stroke Roll 38

    3.C.- Concept Development Part 2 - Dotted Eighth Notes 45

    3.D.- Suggested Patterns 52

Chapter 4: Same Pattern, Different Note Value – Different Ratio 57
4.A.- Concept Introduction - Understanding Polyrhythms Using Unisons 58
4.B.- Concept Development Part 1 - Single Stroke Roll Over Unisons 61
4.C.- Concept Development Part 2 - Suggested Patterns Over a Polyrhythm 67
4.D.- Suggested Polyrhythms 70

Chapter 5: Improvisation Over Ostinatos 73
5.A.- Concept Development Part 1 - Changing Note Values Over an Ostinato 74
5.B.- Concept Development Part 2 - Changing Patterns Over an Ostinato 79
5.C.- Concept Development Part 3 - Groove Development Over an Ostinato 84
5.D.- Concept Development Part 4 - Layered Ostinatos 94

Chapter 6: Using Coordination to Improve Technique 101
6.A.- Concept Development Part 1 - Accents and Flams Over an Ostinato 102
6.B.- Concept Development Part 2 - Accents and Diddles Over an Ostinato 109

Chapter 7: Nested Tuplets 117
7.A.- Concept Introduction - Single Rhythm Nested Tuplets 118
7.B.- Concept Development Part 1 - Different Subdivisions of Nested Tuplets 124
7.C.- Concept Development Part 2 - Rhythmic Combinations of Nested Tuplets 129
7.D.- Suggested Nested Tuplets 131

Chapter 8: Musical Examples and Transcriptions 134
8.A.- Transcription and Analysis and of "Over the Trees" 135
8.B.- Transcription and Analysis of "Travieso" 142

Conclusion 146

Acknowledgments

To my family:

Thank you to my wife, Katie, for inspiring me to be a better musician every day and for patience, love, and support through the years.

Thank you to my brother, Galo, and his wife, Catia, for being the best example anyone could ever ask for. I still want to be like you when I grow up.

Thank you to my parents, Elena and Edgar, for always giving me advice and for trusting and supporting my life choices.

Thank you to my father-in-law, Mike, for sharing a lifetime's worth of musical experience and knowledge.

To my musical family:

Thank you to Jeff Bowders for being an endless source of musical inspiration and for believing in me as a player.

Thank you to Jan Rivera for sharing his knowledge, reviewing the book, and helping me to make this a reality.

Thank you to Biswarup Chattopadhyay for all of the conversations about life and music that make me want to work harder every day.

Thank you to Peter Hume for encouraging and supporting musical ideas that challenge convention.

Additional acknowledgments:

Thank you to Aaron Vishria, Sam Gample, John Farquharson, Steve Bolognese, and all of the current and former TAMA team for their support.

Thank you to Ulf Geist for believing in me as a music educator.

Foreword by Sebastian Lanser

When it comes to drum set coordination and four-limb independence, the possibilities are almost endless. This makes it hard to get a grip and start improving on that topic. In this book Ray provides a great method, which leads you through different concepts and aspects of four-way independence. This book is about building a solid and strong foundation that enables you to explore and master more progressive territories, as there are tons of progressive concepts throughout the book. It also motivates and trains your creative side as you can use the given framework to work on your personal ideas and develop your own voice as an artist. In the end this is the most important part to me – "developing a musical voice" on the instrument and NOT playing exercises while playing music. However, it will take time, focus and patience to reach this ultimate goal. Take your time and go slowly through all of these exercises. Keep in mind that it is the quality and articulation of the execution that matters the most. With careful and ongoing application, results will follow.

Introduction

Welcome to Advanced Drumming Coordination – A Comprehensive Guide to Four-Way Independence.

This book is a comprehensive guide to understanding and developing advanced drumming coordination concepts behind the kit. As you probably know, there are two main subjects that determine our ability to play something behind the kit: technique and coordination. If you are like me, then you have found yourself struggling with the simple things in drumming – like playing a steady quarter note with the hi-hat while playing a groove. Coordination challenges such as this one often affect our ability to play more than we realize. Working through these difficulties as a player is what inspired me to write this book.

The order of the chapters in the book is specifically written to follow an approach that has personally helped me to achieve a proficient level of four-way coordination. I recommend that you work through the book in sequence. When practicing the examples in each chapter, keep in mind that having good coordination and being able to play complex rhythms and patterns with ease is extremely helpful when going back to simpler ideas – like playing a steady quarter note with the hi-hat.

In this book, I walk you through a system that has helped me to gain better balance behind the kit and to better understand how rhythmic patterns relate to each other. Exploring these relationships is a process that takes a lifetime of study because the variations are endless. This system will help you to develop a basic understanding of advanced coordination, broaden your own ideas, expand your vocabulary, and shift your perspective from "independent limbs" to "limbs playing different rhythms together".

Drum Key

For the majority of this book, the examples do not use the standard five-line staff because standard notation makes it much harder to read the examples. To make it easier to read and understand, this book primarily uses a two-line staff.

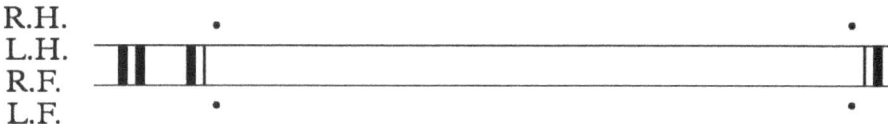

In the staff above, the notes written above the top line represent your right hand (R.H.) and are written as hi-hats. The notes written below the top line represent your left hand (L.H.) and are written as regular note heads. Likewise, the notes written above the bottom line represent your right foot (R.F.) and are written as regular note heads. The notes written below the bottom line represent your left foot (L.F.) and are written as hi-hats. Pay attention to the directions to the left of the staff because the placement of the limbs changes throughout the book.

The Different Combinations

One of the most common limitations when studying coordination is that coordination is often thought of as one-dimensional. This means that we learn how to coordinate a certain pattern(s) with certain limb(s) and then we move onto a different pattern. This leaves many possibilities unexplored. For example, we learn to solo with three limbs over a clave pattern played with our left foot, but not how to solo over the same clave pattern played with the left hand. This book exhausts all of the potential combinations of every pattern with the goal of leaving no possibilities unexplored.

Audio Download

Audio is available for all examples marked with the following symbol:

You can download the audio files at:

https://rayrojodrums.com/adc-audio-files/

Password: adc

• CHAPTER 1 •

Same Pattern, Same Note Value

The first concept we need to understand in order to build a foundation to achieve an advanced level of drumming coordination is: the importance of playing the same pattern, with different limbs, at the same time, using the same note value.

In order to minimize written explanation in this chapter, the examples use familiar rudiments and eighth notes as the common note value.

1.A.- Concept Introduction - Single Stroke Roll

The first rudiment is the single stroke roll. This is the least complicated rudiment to use in a coordination context because it is only a two-note pattern that repeats. Here's what the single stroke roll played with the hands as eighth notes looks like:

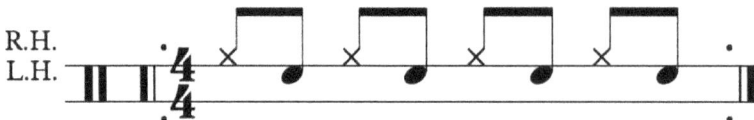

When we add the feet, there are a total of six possible combinations we can play to exhaust all of the four-way coordination possibilities. *It is important to understand that the variations are the result of switching the "leading limb", and not inversions of the pattern.*

1.a.1.

The first possibility is to mirror the pattern with the feet:

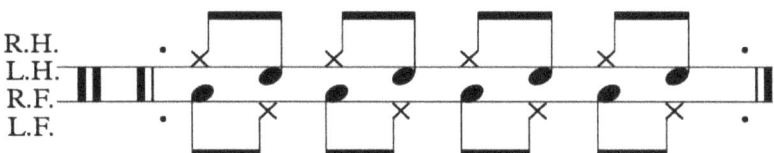

1.a.2.

The second possibility is to keep the hands the same and alter the order of the feet:

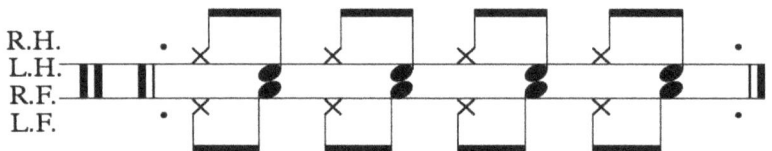

1.a.3.

The third possibility is to switch the hand pattern to mirror the feet:

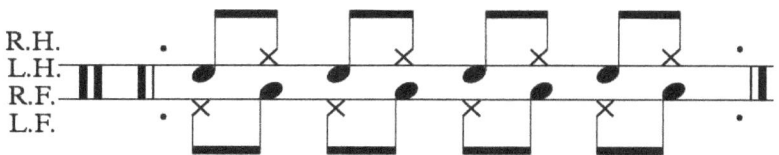

1.a.4.

The fourth possibility is to play the foot pattern from Example 1.a.1. over the hand pattern from Example 1.a.3.:

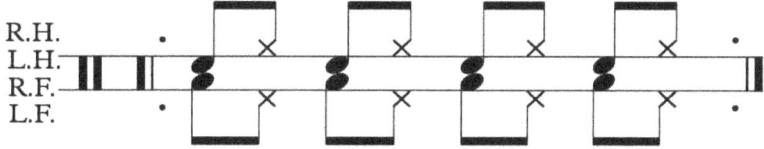

1.a.5.

The fifth possibility is to alter the way that the pattern is organized. Instead of playing the single stroke roll between the hands over the single stroke with the feet, the single stroke roll is now played between the right foot and right hand over the left foot and left hand:

1.a.6.

The sixth and last possibility is to play the same pattern from Example 1.a.5. starting with the hands:

Throughout this process, focus on how your limbs relate to each other. Don't only think "single stroke roll over single stroke roll". For example, pay attention to when the right hand lines up with the left foot, when the left hand lines up with the left foot, or any other possibility you're practicing.

ADVANCED DRUMMING COORDINATION

1.B.- Concept Development Part 1 - Double Stroke Roll

Now, repeat the same steps from section 1.A., but this time use the double stroke roll as the pattern.

1.b.1.

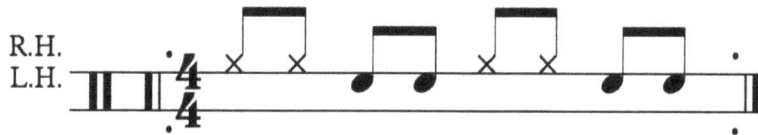

1.b.2.

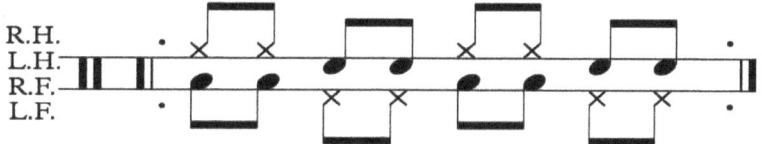

1.b.3.

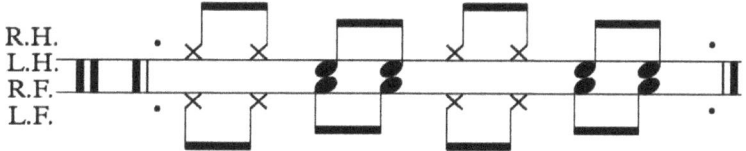

1.b.4.

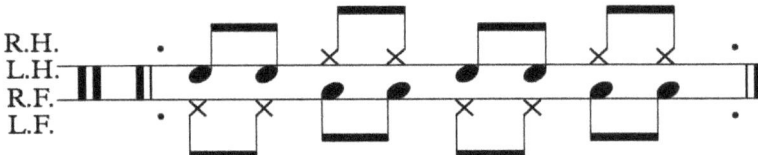

1.b.5.

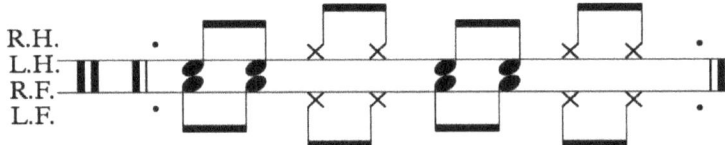

It is important to realize that the number of variations changes based on the length of the patterns.

1.C.- Concept Development Part 2 - Paradiddle

The next pattern, the single paradiddle, is the last one that has all of the variations notated.

1.c.1.

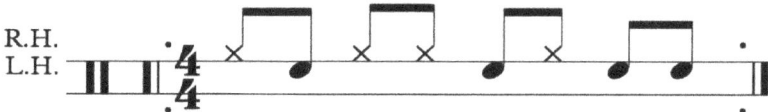

1.c.2.

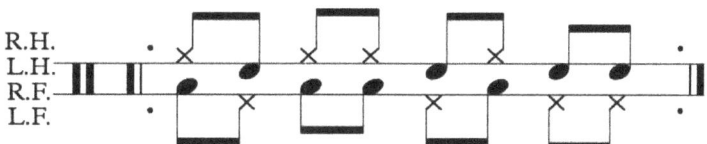

1.c.3.

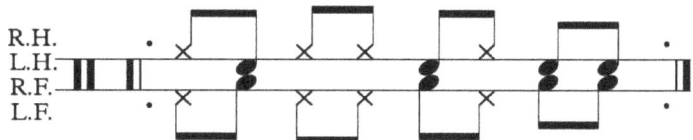

1.c.4.

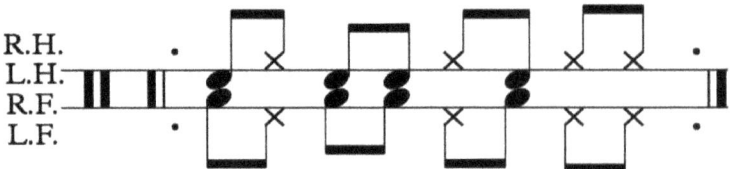

1.c.5.

I encourage you *not* to isolate the hands from the feet. Instead, pay attention to how your limbs relate and learn how it feels for all of your limbs to engage simultaneously. This skill will be very helpful in the later chapters of this book.

1.D.- Suggested Patterns

In this section, I introduce several patterns that you can study in the same way we studied the previous rudiments. The main pattern is included, but the variations are no longer written out. It is up to you to exhaust all of the possibilities. The patterns are not always in 4/4 and not all of the patterns are rudiments.

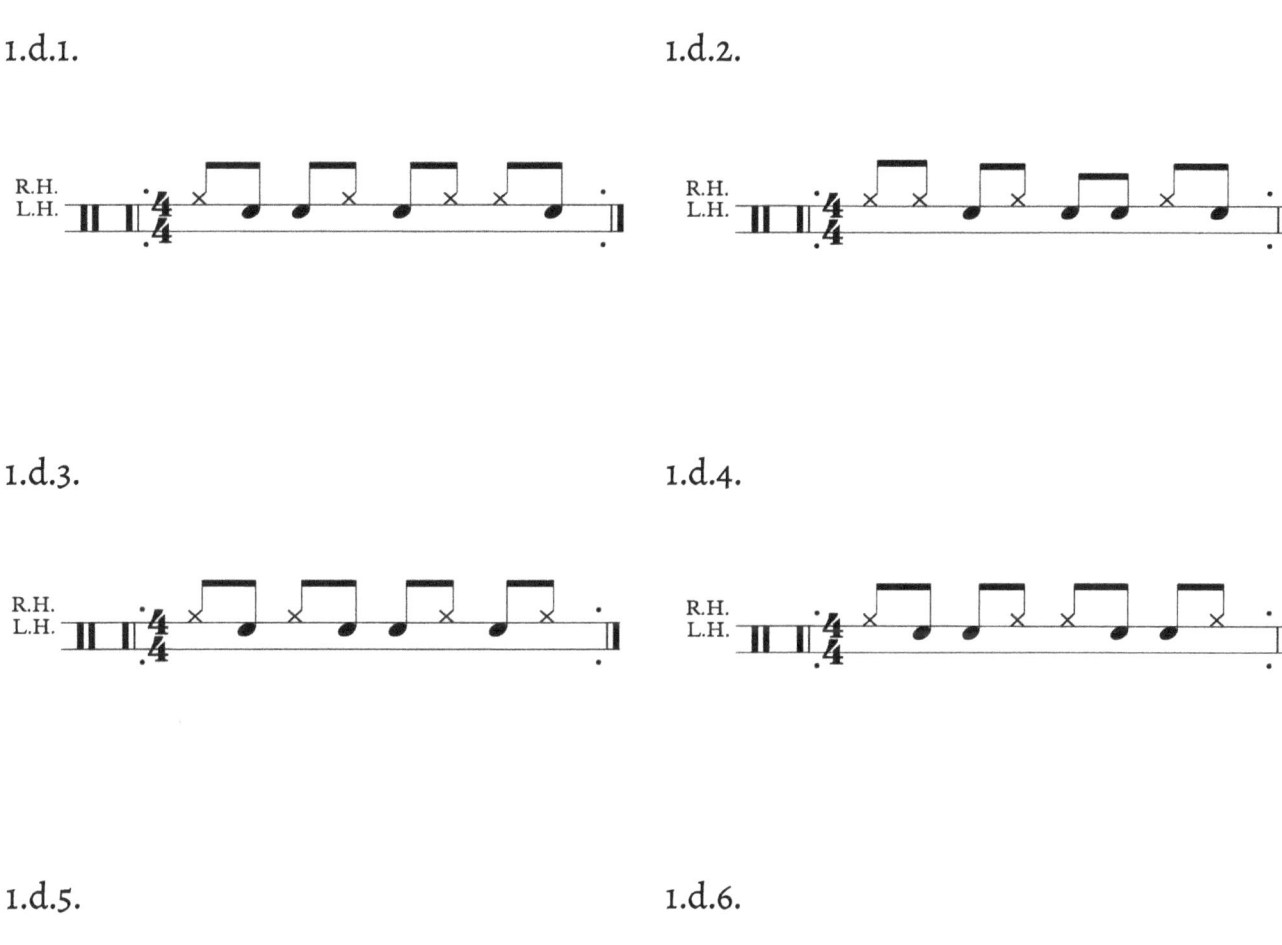

1.d.7.

1.d.8.

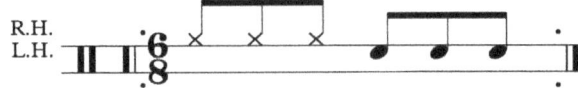

1.d.9.

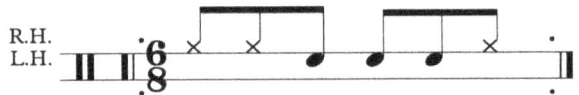

1.d.10.

1.d.11.

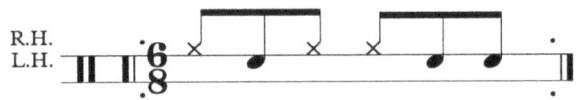

1.d.12.

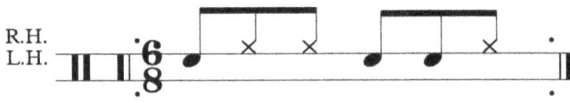

1.d.13.

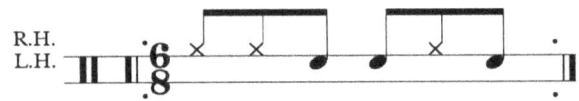

1.d.14.

ADVANCED DRUMMING COORDINATION

1.d.15.   1.d.16.

1.d.17.   1.d.18.

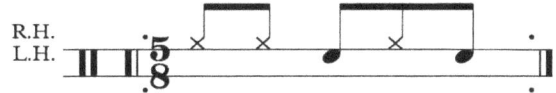   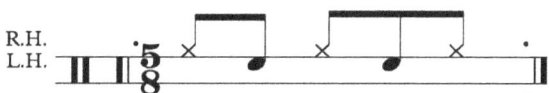

Remember to pay attention to how your limbs relate to each other both within the individual patterns and also as a four-way coordination study.

• CHAPTER 2 •

Coordinating One Voice Over Two-Limb Ostinatos

Now that we've been introduced to four-way independence in chapter one, the next step is to develop the ability to play freely with one limb over a two-limb ostinato. I've found that an effective way to approach freedom over an ostinato is to exhaust all of the possible note groupings over the ostinato first. This gives you a basic understanding of how different rhythms relate to the ostinato, which will be very useful when you add a fourth limb.

This chapter also uses unisons with the two limbs that are not a part of the ostinato, breaking away from the "single limb" topic. However, I encourage you to think of the unison examples as one limb since it is the same rhythm. This is why there are still four-way coordination examples in this chapter.

2.A.- Concept Introduction - Groups of Three as an Ostinato

The ostinato that we start with is a group of three notes played as sixteenth notes.

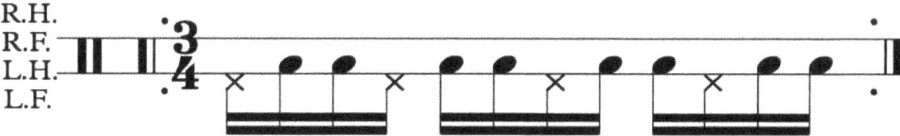

Because it is a three-note pattern played over sixteenth notes, it is written in 3/4. If we were to play the ostinato in 4/4, it would take three bars for the pattern to restart. In this section, the time signatures change to ensure that both the pattern being played with the single limb and the ostinato come back around in just one bar. This will affect your counting system but will make it easier to learn because the phrases will always be represented in their shortest form.

2.a.1.

The first possibility is to simply play all of the sixteenth notes in unison with the ostinato.

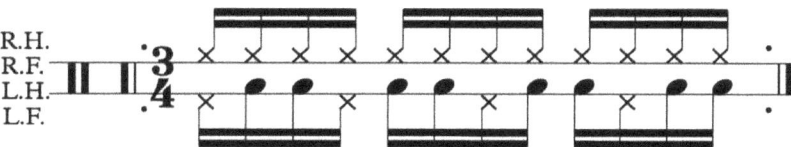

2.a.2.

Repeat the same rhythm with the other limb that is not a part of the ostinato.

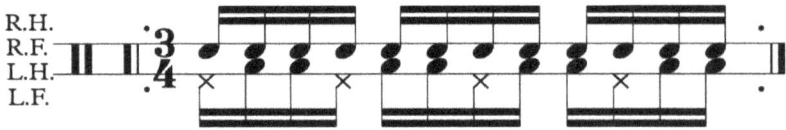

2.a.3.

Play both limbs in unison.

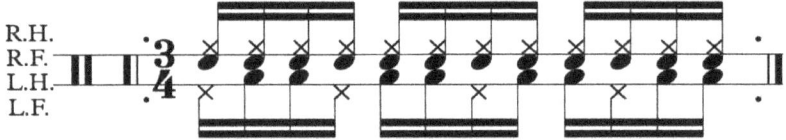

2.a.4.

The next step is to play every other note – or groups of two – in the pattern, which is the same as playing eighth notes.

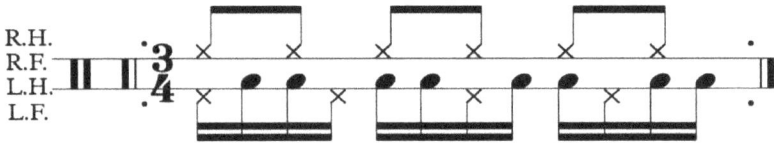

2.a.5.

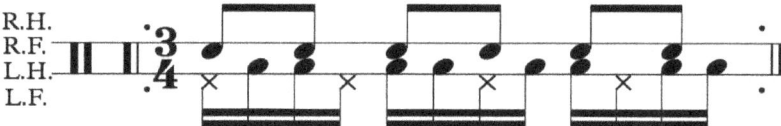

2.a.6.

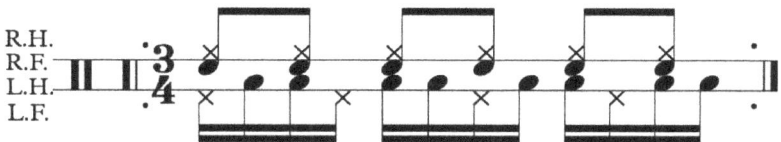

2.a.7.

The next step is to play every three notes – or groups of three – over the ostinato, which is the same as playing a dotted eighth note and will, in this case, line up with the left foot.

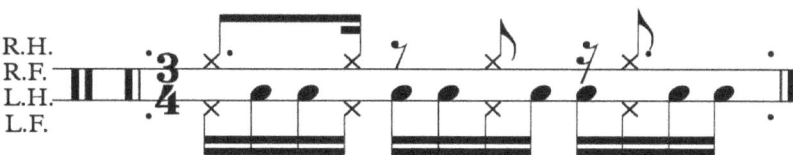

2.a.8.

2.a.9.

2.a.10.

The next step is to play every four notes – or groups of four – over the ostinato, which is the same as playing a quarter note.

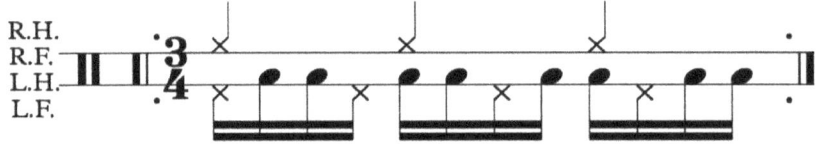

2.a.11.

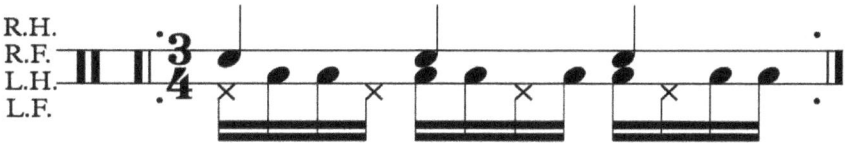

2.a.12.

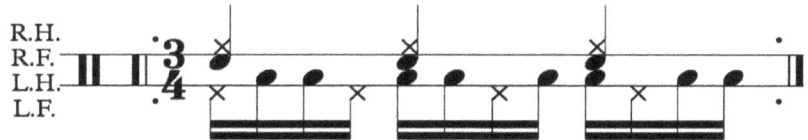

2.a.13.

The next possibility is to play every five sixteenth notes – or groups of five – over the ostinato. Note that in order for the pattern to come back around in one bar, the time signature has been changed to 15/8.

2.a.14.

2.a.15.

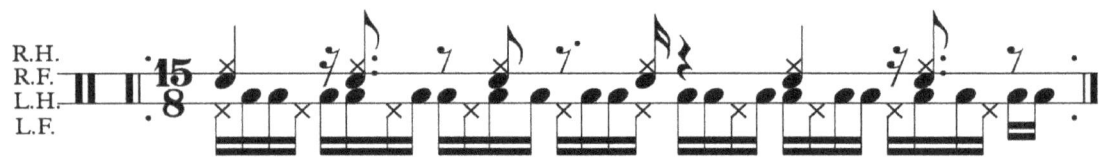

2.a.16.

The next step is to play every six sixteenth notes – or groups of six – over the ostinato. Note that the time signature is back to 3/4.

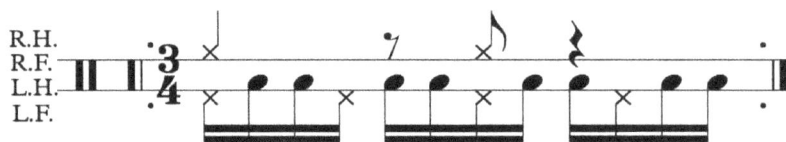

2.a.17.

2.a.18.

2.a.19.

The next step is to play every seven sixteenth notes – or groups of seven – over the ostinato. Note that the time signature has changed to 21/8.

2.a.20.

2.a.21.

2.a.22.

The last step in this section is to play every eight sixteenth notes – or groups of eight – over the ostinato, which is the same as a half note. Note that the time signature has changed to 6/4.

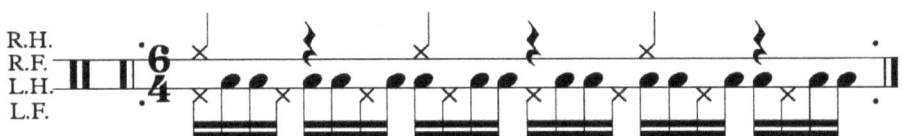

2.a.23.

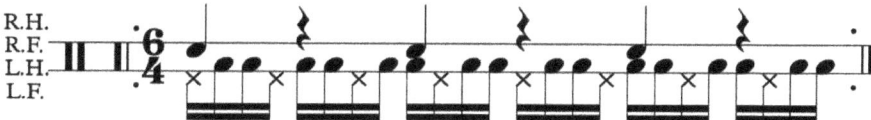

2.a.24.

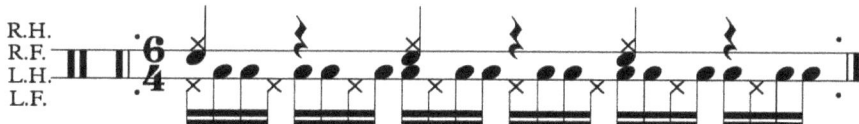

Before moving on, remember that there are many more possible combinations with this ostinato alone. This idea can be played, for example, with the ostinato between the hands and the groupings with the feet, or the ostinato between your left foot and right hand and the groupings with the right foot and left hand, etc. Remember that it is up to you to exhaust all of the possibilities. You can also continue and include groups of nine, eleven, or any other grouping you would like.

2.a.25.

The hardest things to play are always transitions. It doesn't matter if it is in a song or in a set of examples like the ones above; transitions are always difficult to play. The ultimate goal is to be able to transition between different sections with ease.

The next example combines the previous eight variations to create a complete coordination workout over groups of three. The two limbs that are not part of the ostinato are playing in unison at all times and each grouping is played for two full bars.

2.B.- Concept Development Part 1 - Rhythmic Ideas Over the Ostinato

The same steps can be followed to explore different rhythmic ideas over ostinatos. We can change the rhythms to accentuate groupings of three, four, five, and so on in different ways over any ostinato. This section provides common rhythmic patterns for the groupings that we used in the previous section.

For the sake of simplicity, the examples are written over the same three-note ostinato and in the same time signatures used in the previous section of this chapter. Please note that only one of the three combinations is written – only the right hand – and it is up to you to exhaust all of the possibilities.

2.b.1.

The following examples are different rhythms that can be used to play groups of three.

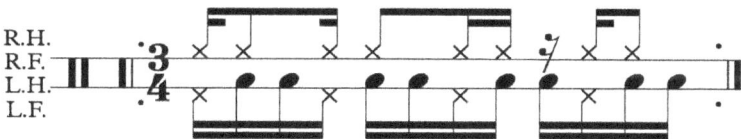

2.b.2.

This example displaces the rhythm from the previous example by one sixteenth note.

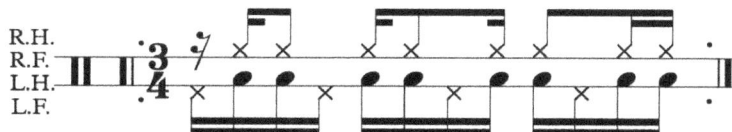

2.b.3.

The following examples are different rhythms that can be used to play groups of four.

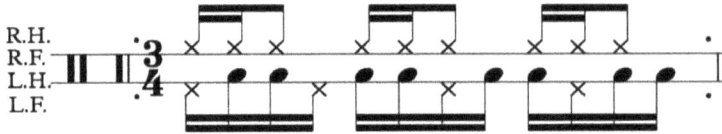

2.b.4.

2.b.5.

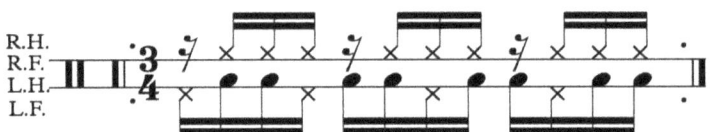

ADVANCED DRUMMING COORDINATION

2.b.6.

The following examples are different rhythms that can be used to play groups of five.

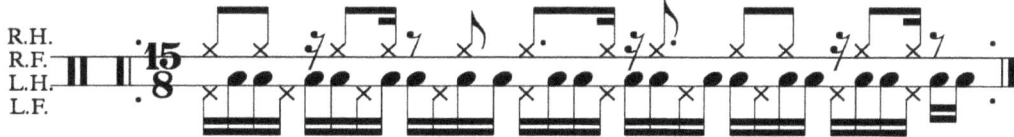

2.b.7.

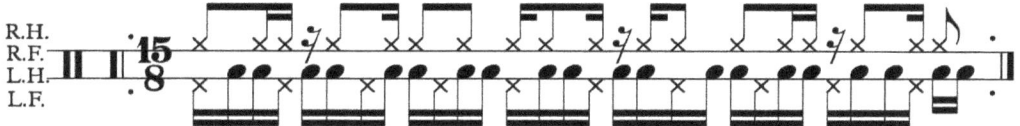

2.b.8.

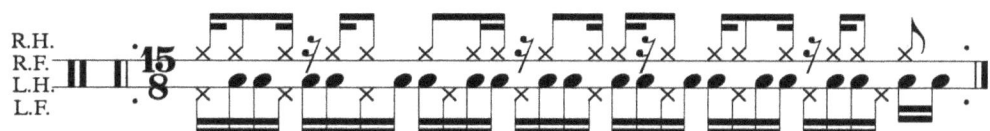

2.b.9.

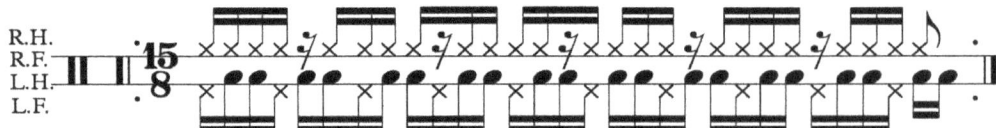

2.b.10.

The following examples are different rhythms that can be used to play groups of seven.

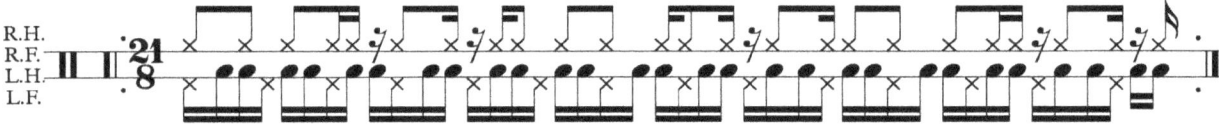

2.b.11.

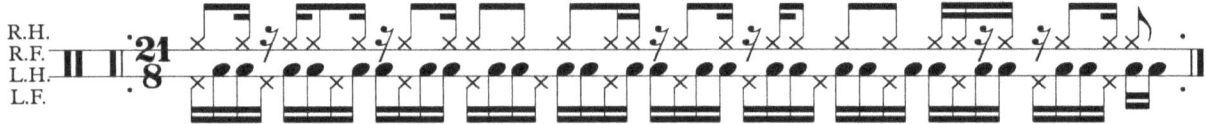

It is important to feel comfortable with the previous examples before moving on to the next chapter. They will help you to build the coordination necessary to be able to play the examples in the following chapters.

Remember to always count out loud and to practice with a metronome.

2.C.- Concept Development Part 2 - Modifying the Ostinato

This section modifies the examples in the previous section from three-limb coordination to four-limb coordination exercises by doubling one of the limbs that plays the ostinato. This adds a new layer of coordination while continuing to play three rhythms. For example, we can play the right foot in unison with the left foot, turning the ostinato alone into a three-limb pattern.

2.c.1.

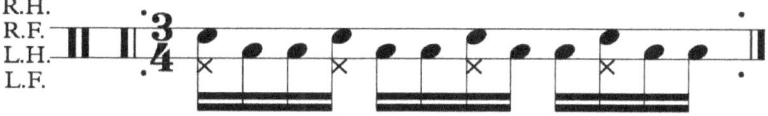

2.c.2.

The following example doubles the left foot of the ostinato with the right hand.

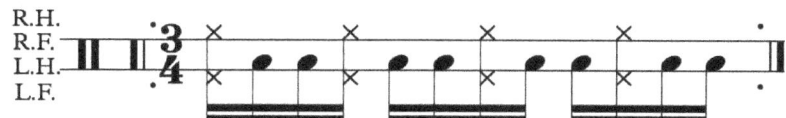

2.c.3.

The following example doubles the left hand of the ostinato with the right foot.

2.c.4.

The following example doubles the left hand of the ostinato with the right hand.

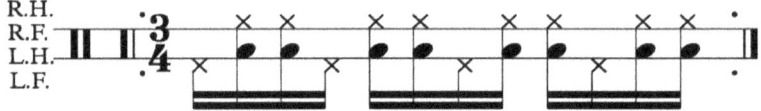

2.c.5.

The next few examples demonstrate some of the previous three-limb ostinato variations over some of the rhythmic patterns from section 2.B.

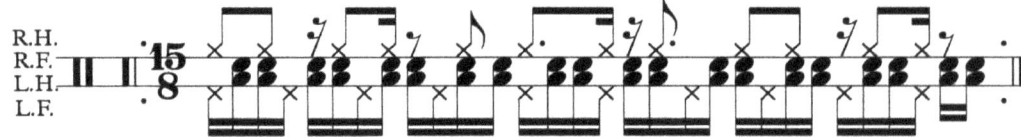

ADVANCED DRUMMING COORDINATION

2.c.6.

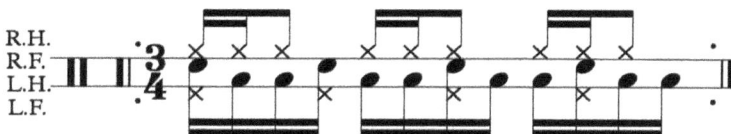

2.c.7.

2.c.8.

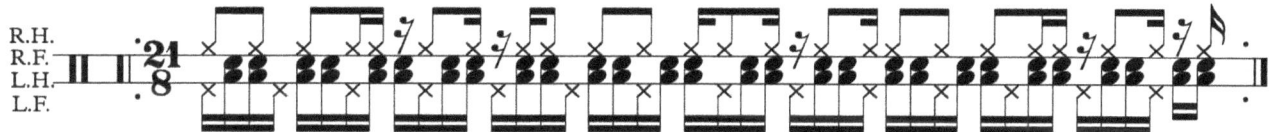

Once again, I encourage you to exhaust all of the possibilities. Remember that you can play the same examples, but instead of playing the ostinato in unison with the bass drum, you can play it with the right hand and play the different rhythms with the bass drum.

• CHAPTER 3 •

Same Pattern, Different Note Value – Same Ratio

The next step to achieve an advanced level of drumming coordination is to play one pattern with two limbs over the same pattern with the other two limbs using a different note value. This creates a more complex coordination challenge because it combines two rhythms and alters the way the pattern fits within itself. This can also make the phrases considerably longer, which inherently makes them harder to play and adds more variations, which means the same pattern can be studied in several more ways.

It is important to understand that this chapter uses different note values that are in the same ratio. This means that even though we are playing different note values, the note values still directly relate to each other and both line up and fit within the same counting system. For example, you can count sixteenth notes (1-e-and-a) and play eighth notes (1-and) and the "1" and the "and" will always line up. In contrast, this alignment does not occur when you play eighth notes and eighth note triplets because they are in a different ratio.

In the first section of this chapter, we play the same patterns as in chapter one, but two limbs will play the pattern as sixteenth notes and two limbs will play the same pattern as eighth notes.

3.A.- Concept Introduction - Single Stroke Roll

As in Chapter 1, the first pattern is the single stroke roll.

3.a.1.

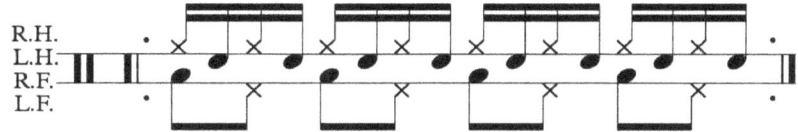

3.a.2.

3.a.3.

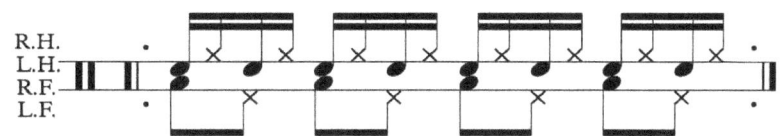

3.a.4.

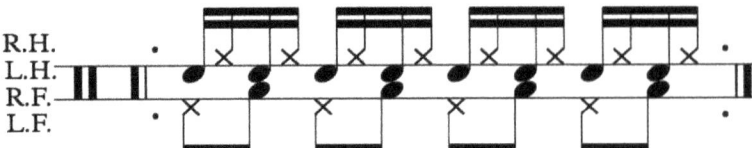

3.a.5.

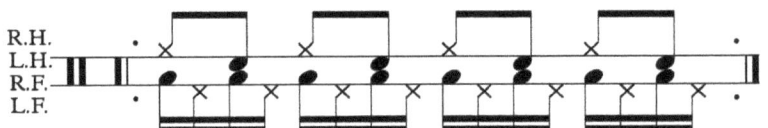

3.a.6.

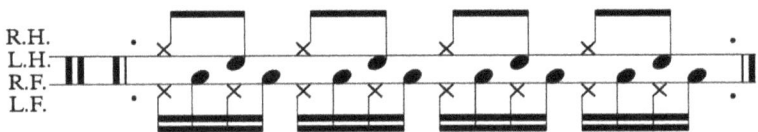

3.a.7.

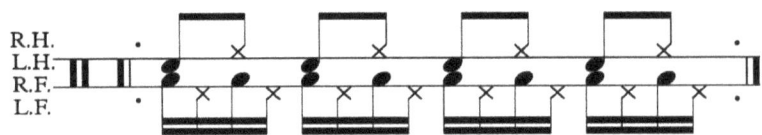

3.a.8.

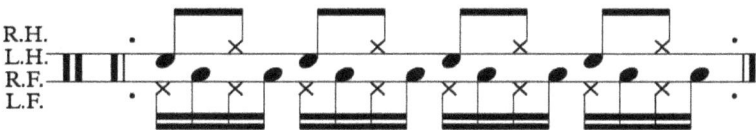

3.a.9.

3.a.10.

3.a.11.

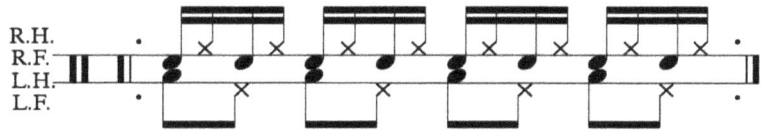

3.a.12.

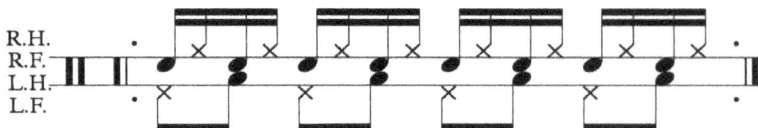

3.a.13.

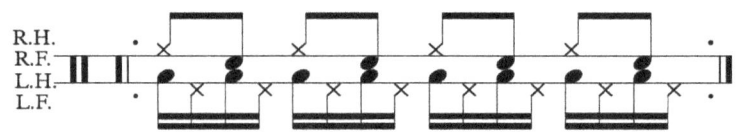

3.a.14.

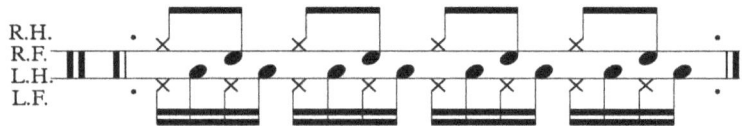

3.a.15.

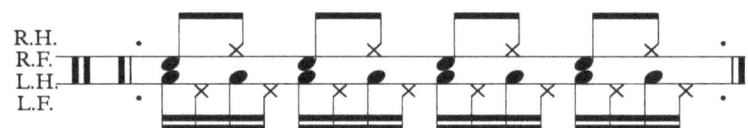

3.a.16.

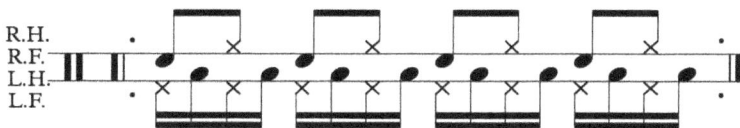

3.a.17.

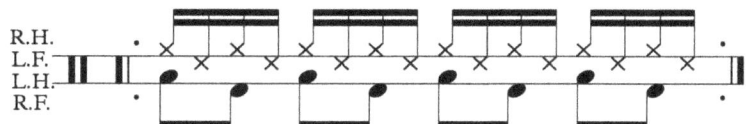

3.a.18.

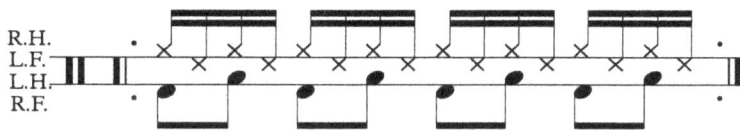

3.a.19.

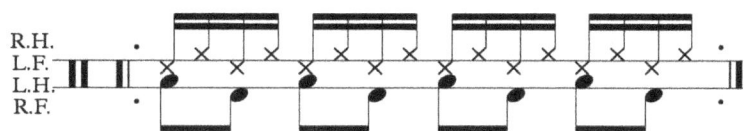

3.a.20.

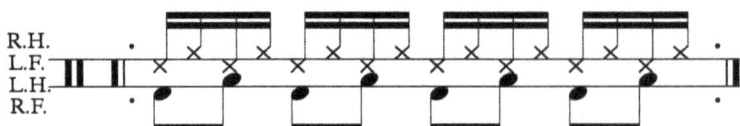

3.a.21.

3.a.22.

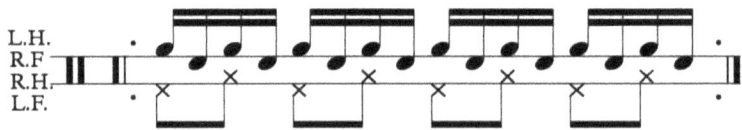

3.a.23.

3.a.24.

3.B.- Concept Development Part 1 - Double Stroke Roll

We now repeat the same steps as in section 1.B., using the double stroke roll as our pattern.

3.b.1.

3.b.2.

3.b.3.

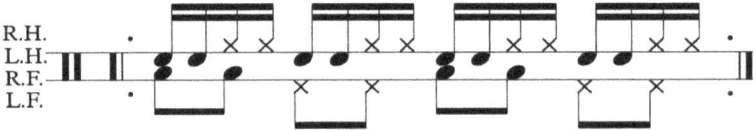

3.b.4.

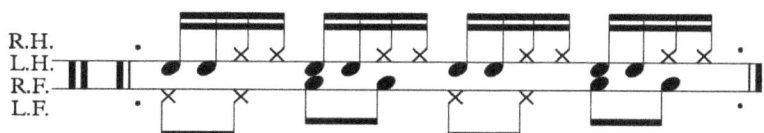

3.b.5.
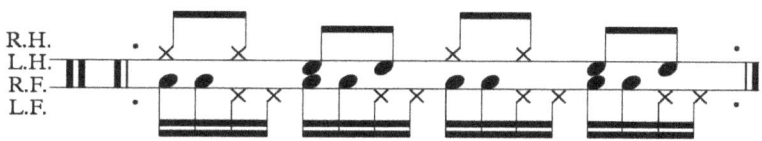

3.b.6.
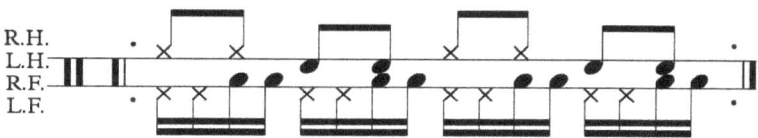

3.b.7.
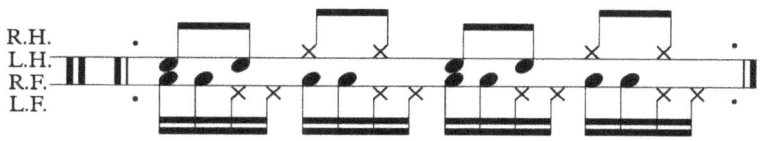

3.b.8.

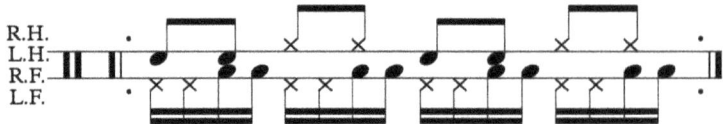

3.b.9.

3.b.10.

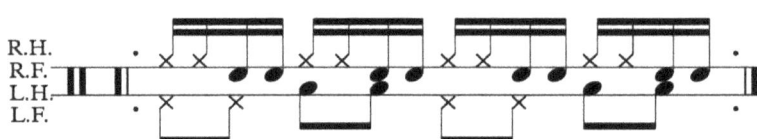

3.b.11.

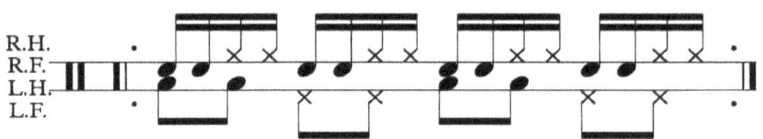

3.b.12.

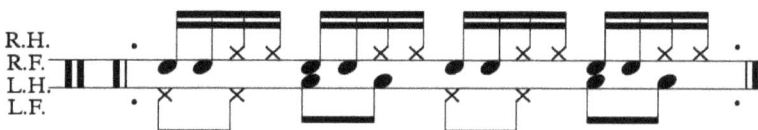

3.b.13.

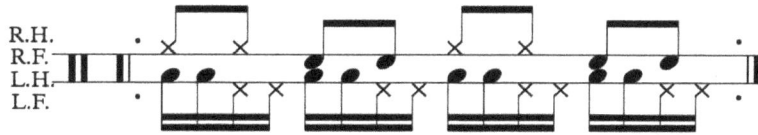

3.b.14.

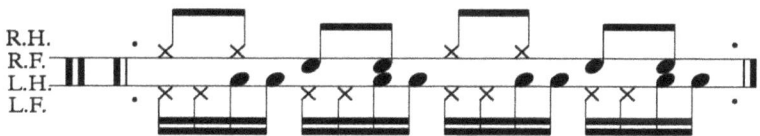

3.b.15.

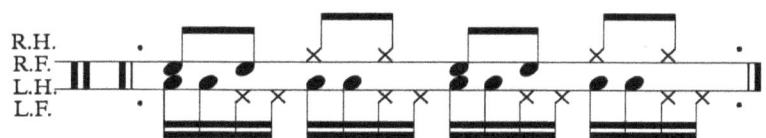

3.b.16.

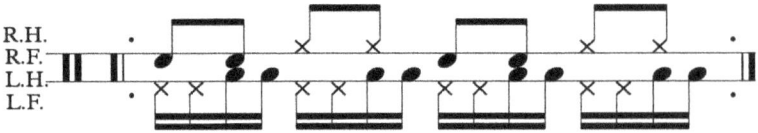

3.b.17.

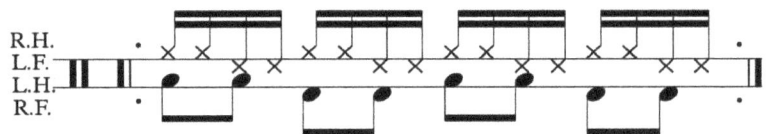

3.b.18.

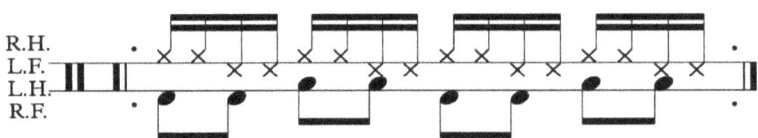

3.b.19.

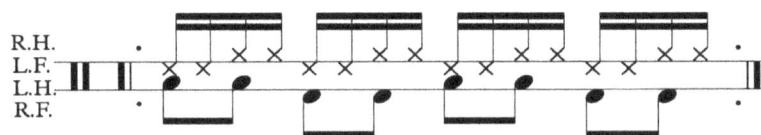

3.b.20.

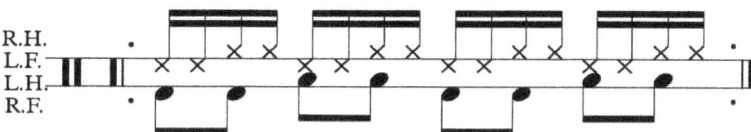

3.b.21.

3.b.22.

3.b.23.

3.b.24.

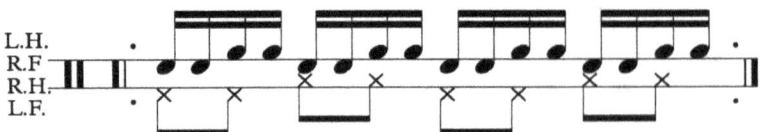

3.C.- Concept Development Part 2 - Dotted Eighth Notes

In this section, we continue playing sixteenth note patterns with two limbs but change the eighth note patterns to dotted eighth notes. This creates a polyrhythm of 4:3, extends the phrases, and completely changes the sound of the patterns.

When playing polyrhythms, it is crucial to count through each example. Without counting, it is possible that your ears will hold onto the groups of three (played by the dotted eighth notes) as a "new quarter note", which will then cause you to lose the original pulse. Counting always prevents this from happening.

The time signatures are altered in order to play the patterns as one-bar phrases. You, of course, may alter this and learn to play them in 4/4 as well.

3.c.1.

In this section, the pattern is the single paradiddle.

3.c.2.

3.c.3.

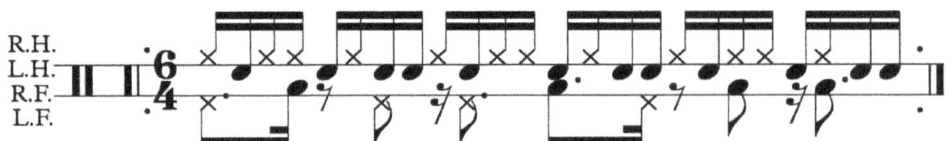

3.c.4.

3.c.5.

3.c.6.

3.c.7.

3.c.8.

3.c.9.

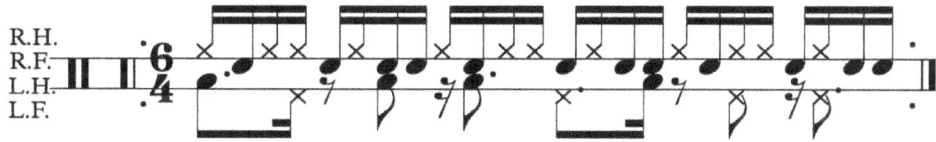

3.c.10.

3.c.11.

3.c.12.

3.c.13.

3.c.14.

3.c.15.

3.c.16.

3.c.17.

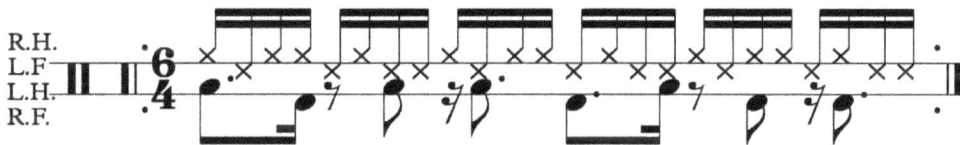

3.c.18.

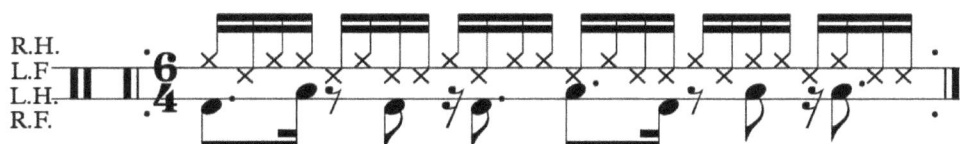

3.C.19.

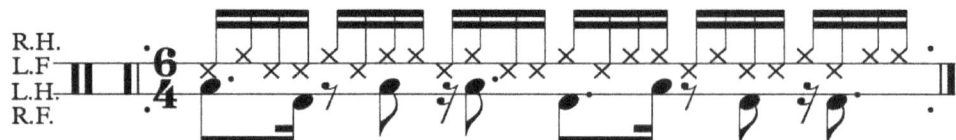

3.C.20.

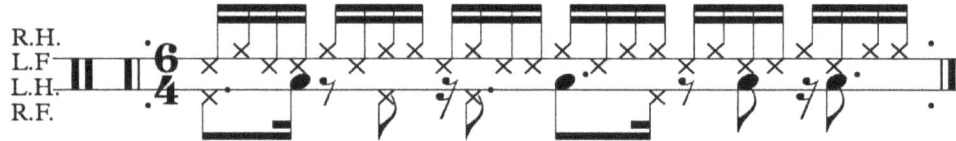

3.C.21.

3.C.22.

3.c.23.

3.c.24.

3.D.- Suggested Patterns

This section presents several rhythmic ideas and groupings that can be played over any pattern. For the sake of simplicity, the ideas are written over the single stroke roll. Remember that you can play any of these rhythmic ideas over any of the examples previously used in this book as well as any additional ideas you have.

As in chapter one, the main idea is written, but the variations are no longer included. It is again up to you to exhaust all of the possibilities. I invite you to refer to section 1.D. and utilize those patterns for reference. As you have probably noticed, the possibilities are endless.

3.d.1.

The following examples demonstrate different ways to play groups of three with two limbs, an extension of the dotted eighth note pattern.

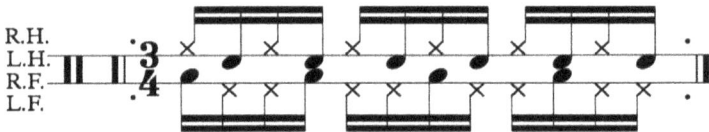

3.d.2.

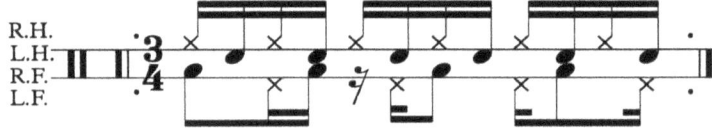

3.d.3.

3.d.4.

Now, the next examples demonstrate different ways to play groups of five with two limbs.

3.d.5.

3.d.6.

3.d.7.

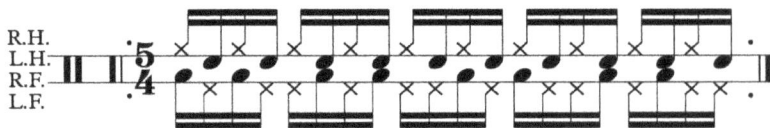

3.d.8.

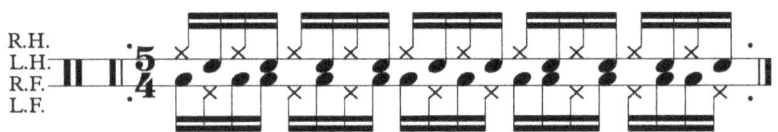

3.d.9.

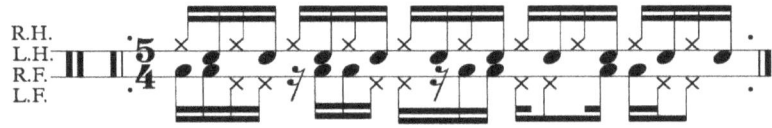

3.d.10.

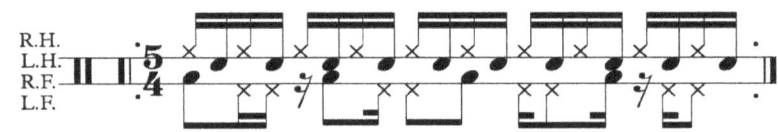

3.d.11.

The next set of examples demonstrate different ways to play groups of seven with two limbs.

3.d.12.

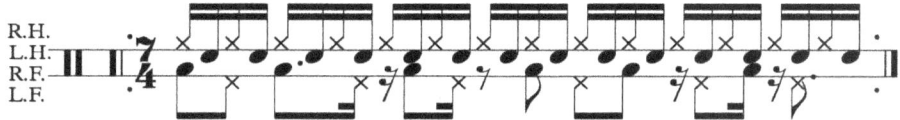

3.d.13.

3.d.14.

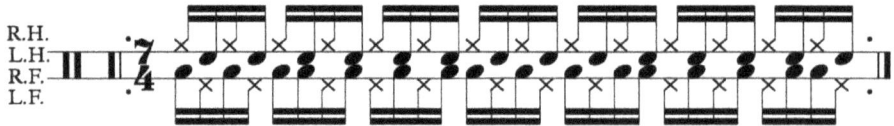

3.d.15.

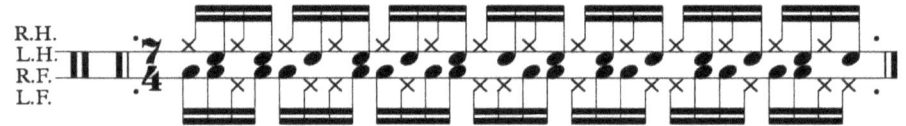

ADVANCED DRUMMING COORDINATION

• CHAPTER 4 •

Same Pattern, Different Note Value– Different Ratio

The rhythmic concepts in this chapter are considerably more complicated than in the previous three chapters. So far, the ideas have had the same underlying subdivision (same ratio) – for example, eighth notes and sixteenth notes – so even if the notes have different values, they can be evenly subdivided and the rhythmic concepts are not too complex.

Notes Align

However, when you switch the underlying subdivision of one of the patterns to a different ratio – for example, triplets over eighth notes – a polyrhythm is created. The ideas no longer align and not all notes are played in unison. This creates two challenges: it is much harder to count through the examples because there are two different subdivisions being played simultaneously and it can extend the length of the phrases.

Notes Don't Align

4.A.- Concept Introduction - Understanding Polyrhythms Using Unisons

In order to be able to play two patterns with two different note values, we first need to understand the polyrhythm that is being played. In the first section of this chapter, we use a polyrhythm of 3:2, which is created when we play quarter notes against quarter note triplets or eighth notes against eighth note triplets. In this section, we use the eighth note against eighth note triplet to create the polyrhythm.

4.a.1.

The first step is to play the polyrhythm with only two limbs.

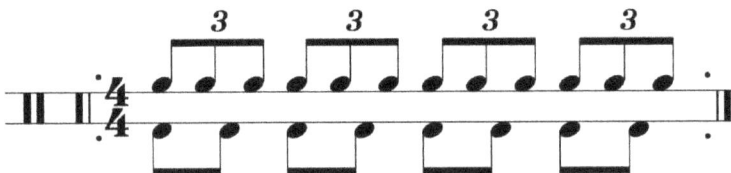

Note that there is no specific hand or foot selected for either of the rhythms. Practice all of the possible combinations two limbs at a time. Learn to hear the relationship between the two note values by switching the counting system back and forth while continuously playing. *Always practice to a metronome!*

4.a.2.

The next step is to play two limbs in unison against the other two limbs in unison. For clarity, the variations are notated.

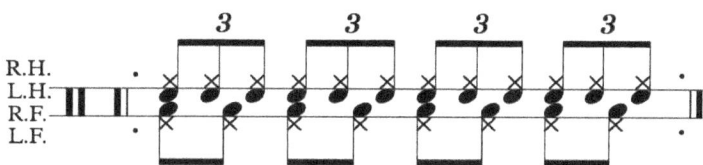

4.a.3.

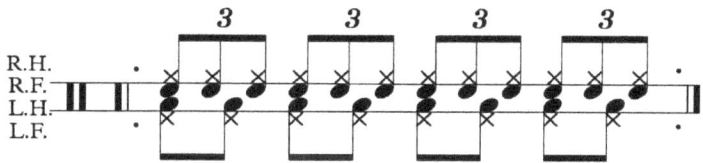

4.a.4.

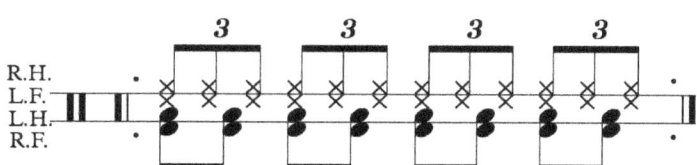

4.a.5.

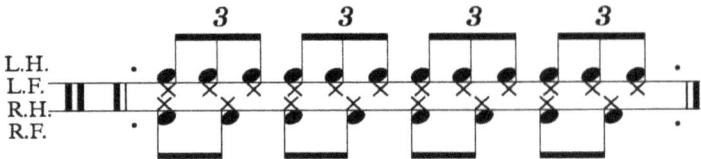

4.a.6.

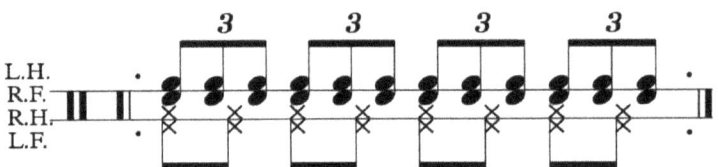

4.a.7.

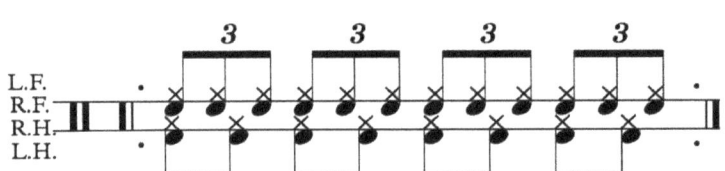

ADVANCED DRUMMING COORDINATION

4.B.- Concept Development Part 1 - Single Stroke Roll Over Unisons

When you feel comfortable with the previous section and understand the sound and relationship of the polyrhythm, it is time to separate two of the limbs into a different pattern. Because the rhythmic content is more complicated than it has been in the previous three chapters, there are more steps included to help you understand the polyrhythm.

4.b.1.

As before, the first pattern is the single stroke roll. Start by playing singles with the hands as eighth note triplets over unison eighth notes with the feet.

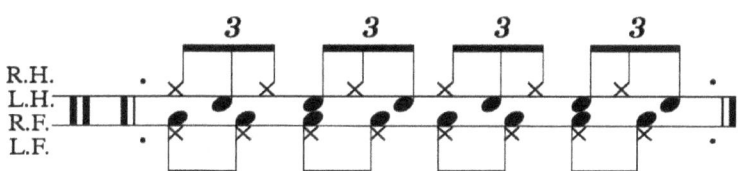

4.b.2.

The next step is to switch the leading hand of the single stroke roll.

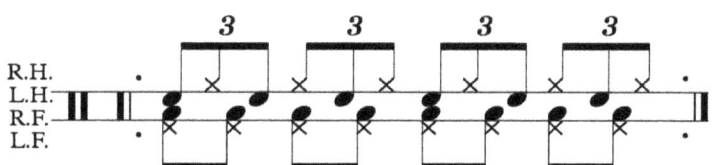

4.b.3.

Now play the single stroke roll with the feet as eighth note triplets and play eighth note unisons with the hands.

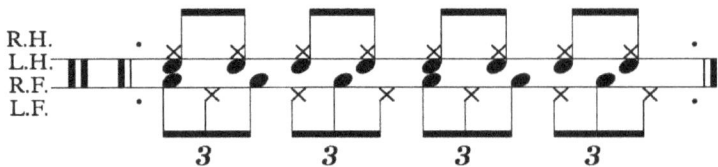

4.b.4.

The next step is to change the leading foot.

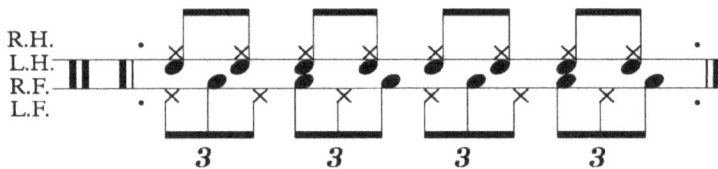

4.b.5.

Now start crossing limbs by playing the single stroke roll as eighth note triplets between the right hand and the left foot over eighth notes in unison between the right foot and left hand.

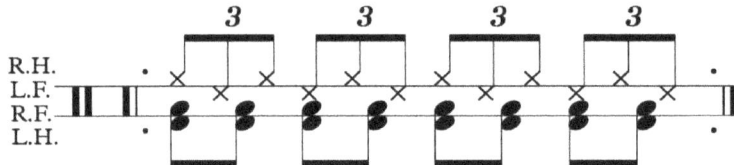

4.b.6.

The next step is to switch the leading limb of the single stroke roll.

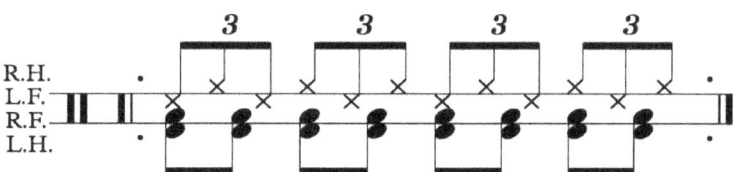

4.b.7.

Now play the single stroke roll as eighth note triplets between the right foot and the left hand over eighth notes as unison between the right hand and left foot.

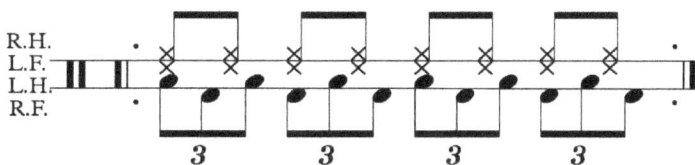

4.b.8.

Now switch the leading limb of the single stroke roll.

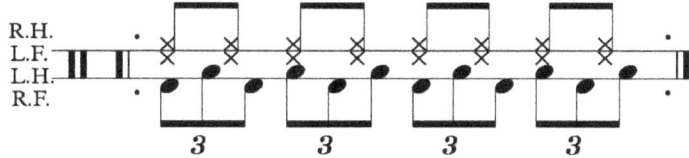

4.b.9.

Once you are comfortable playing the single stroke roll as eighth note triplets, repeat the previous examples but this time play the eighth note triplets as unisons and the single stroke roll as eighth notes.

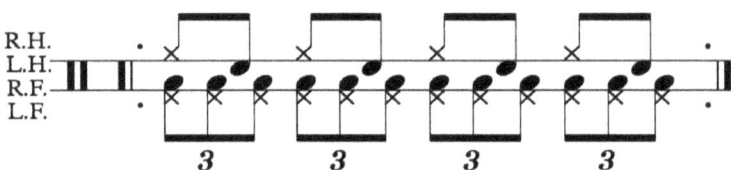

4.b.10.

Switch the leading hand.

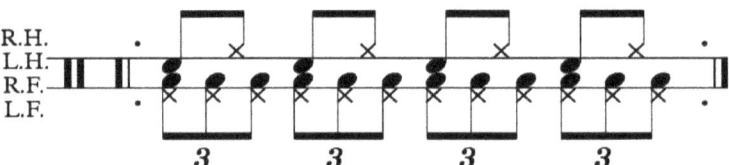

4.b.11.

Play the single stroke roll as eighth notes with the feet.

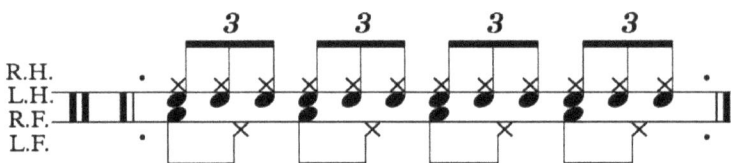

4.b.12.

Switch the leading foot of the single stroke roll.

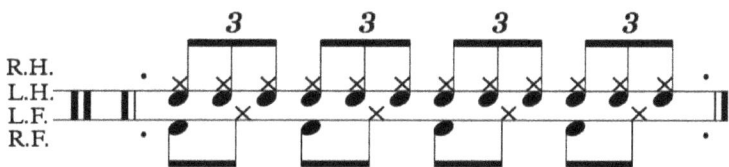

4.b.13.

As before, the next step is to cross the limbs that play the single stroke roll. Start by playing the single stroke roll between the right hand and the left foot as eighth notes over unison eighth note triplets between the right foot and left hand.

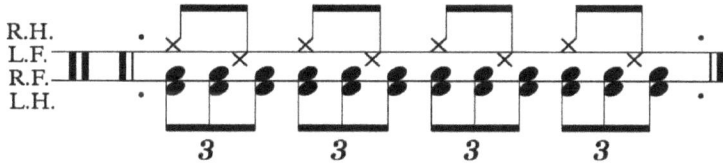

4.b.14.

Switch the leading limb of the single stroke roll.

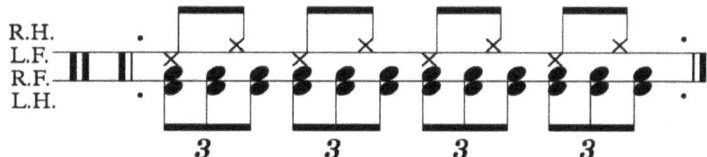

4.b.15.

Now play the single stroke roll as eighth notes between the right foot and the left hand over unison eighth note triplets between the right hand and the left foot.

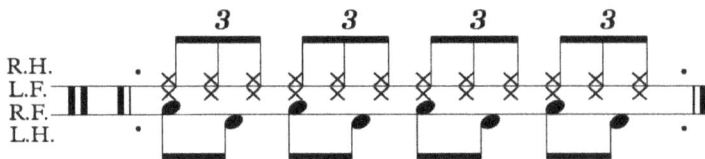

4.b.16.

The last step is to switch the leading limb of the single stroke roll.

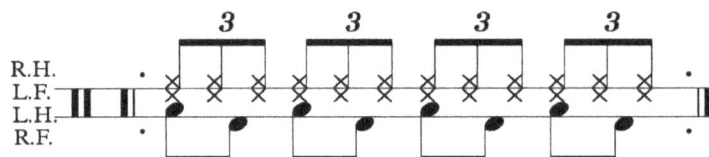

As you have likely noticed by now, the difference in difficulty between this chapter and the previous three chapters is significant. Please do not skip the first three chapters! They are the building blocks that develop the coordination necessary to successfully play ideas like the ones presented in this chapter.

ADVANCED DRUMMING COORDINATION

4.C.- Concept Development Part 2 - Suggested Patterns Over a Polyrhythm

This section provides several ideas that can be used to continue to develop your coordination skills using the same polyrhythm of 3:2. Again, the variations are no longer written out and it is up to you to exhaust all of the possibilities.

4.c.1.

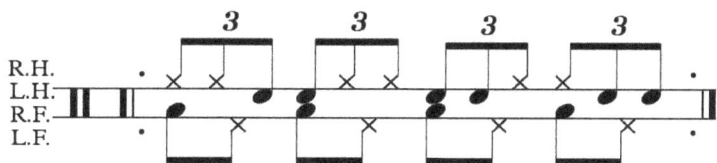

4.c.2.

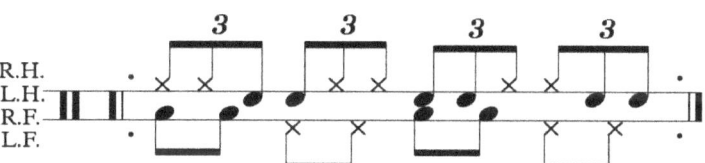

4.c.3.

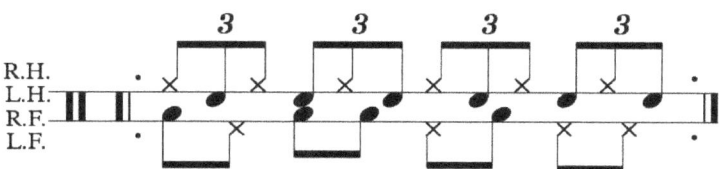

4.c.4.

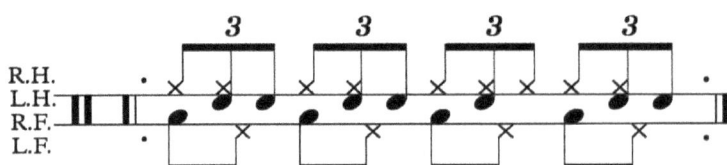

4.c.5.

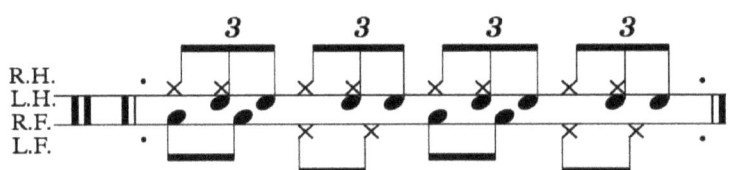

4.c.6.

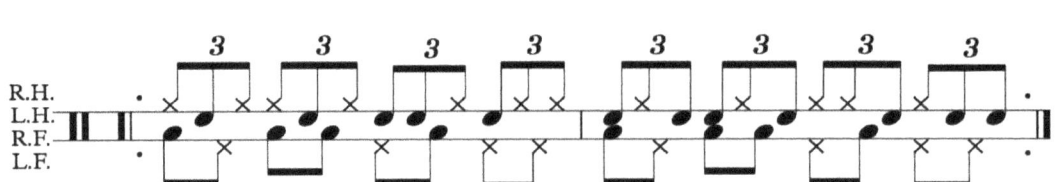

4.c.7.

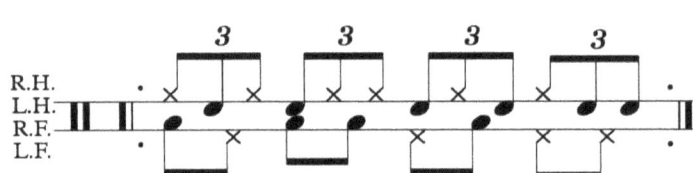

4.c.8.

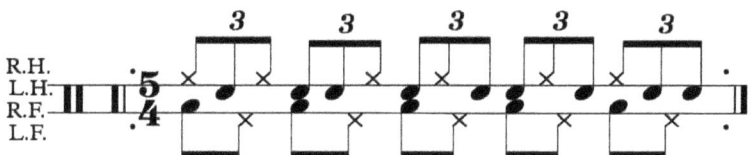

4.c.9.

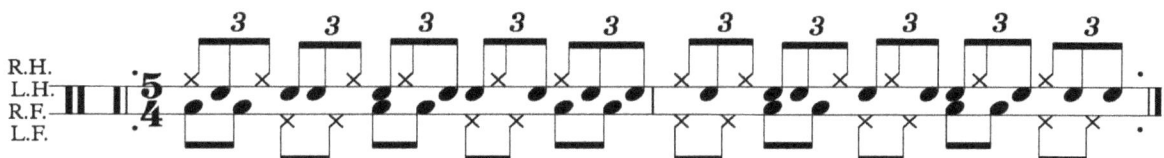

4.D.- Suggested Polyrhythms

The world of rhythmic possibilities is endless as are the different combinations of rhythms and patterns between our four limbs. To conclude this chapter, several more polyrhythms are provided that can be used to continue to expand vocabulary and coordination skills.

The examples do not have specific limbs assigned and there are no variations written. The purpose is to challenge you to exhaust the possibilities on your own. This process leads you to create and find your own patterns and encourages the development of your own voice.

4.d.1.

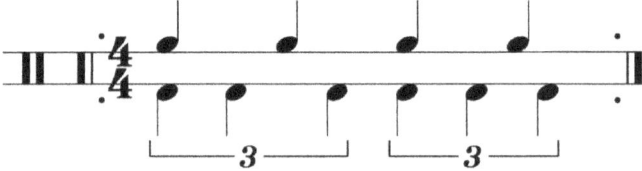

4.d.2.

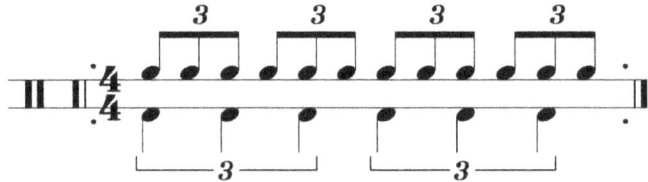

4.d.3.

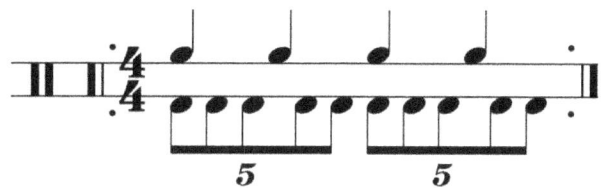

4.d.4.

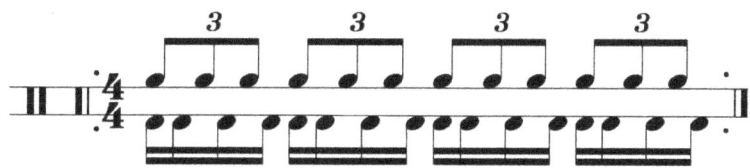

4.d.5.

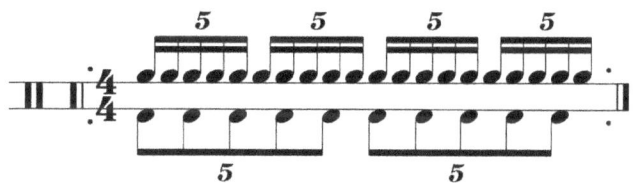

4.d.6.

RAY ROJO

4.d.7.

• CHAPTER 5 •

Improvisation Over Ostinatos

The previous four chapters have built a strong foundation. Your rhythmic understanding and coordination are now at a level that allows you to explore ideas that are much more musical and practical. In this chapter, we begin to apply these ideas to work toward the ultimate goal: improvisation.

5.A.- Concept Development Part 1 - Changing Note Values Over an Ostinato

The first step to improvise over an ostinato is, of course, to set an ostinato. I encourage you to write your own ostinatos to start developing your own voice behind the kit. Remember that an ostinato can be played by one, two or three limbs. In this chapter, we use a two-limb ostinato as an example.

5.a.1.

To begin improvising over an ostinato, switch the note value of the pattern that is played over the ostinato. For the sake of simplicity, the ostinato is the single paradiddle played with the feet as sixteenth notes in 4/4 and the pattern played with the hands is the single stroke roll.

Now repeat the same idea with several different hand patterns.

5.a.2.

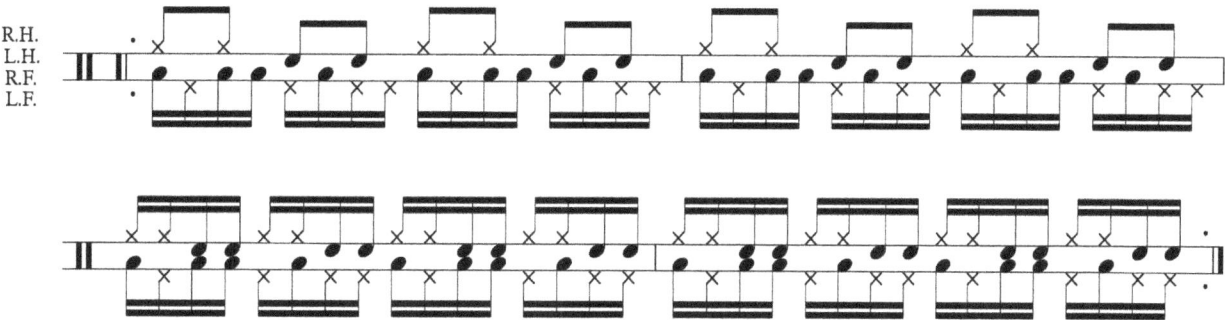

5.a.3.

5.a.4.

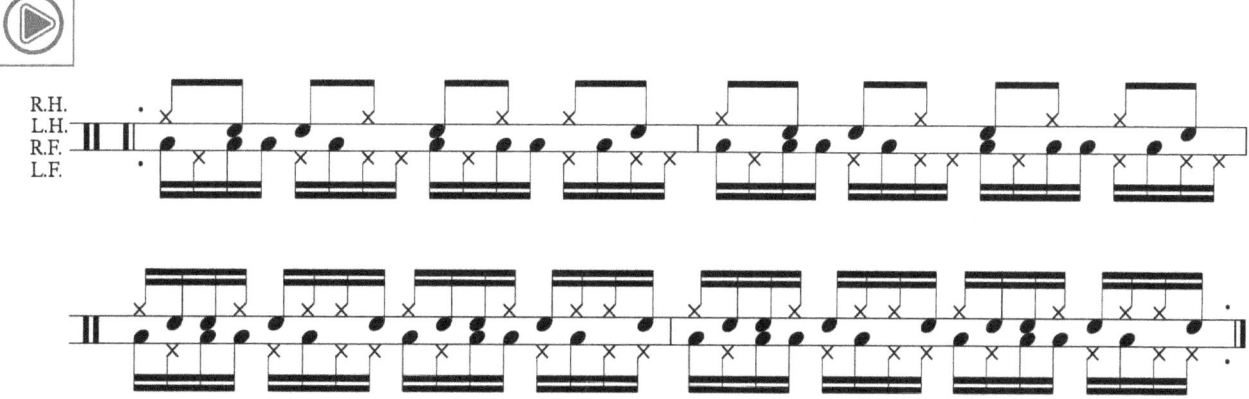

5.a.5.

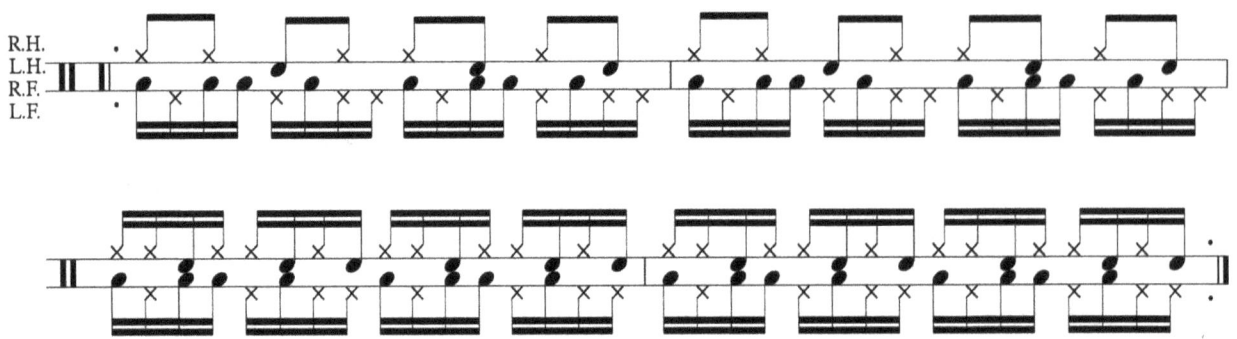

5.a.6.

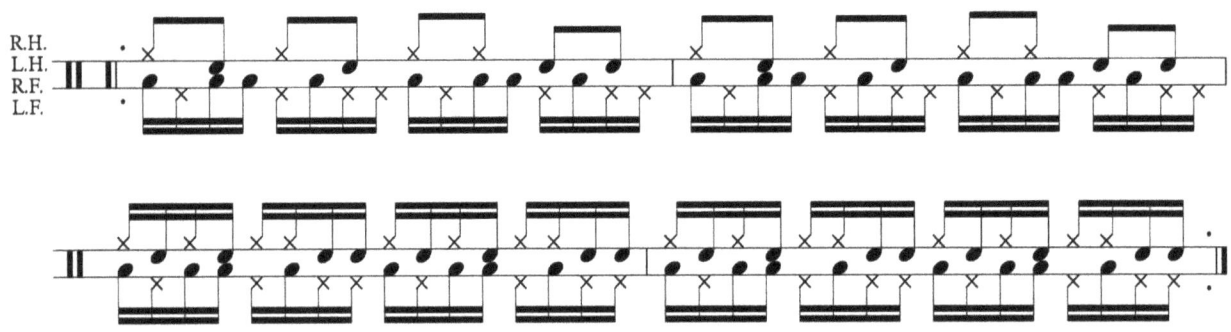

5.a.7.

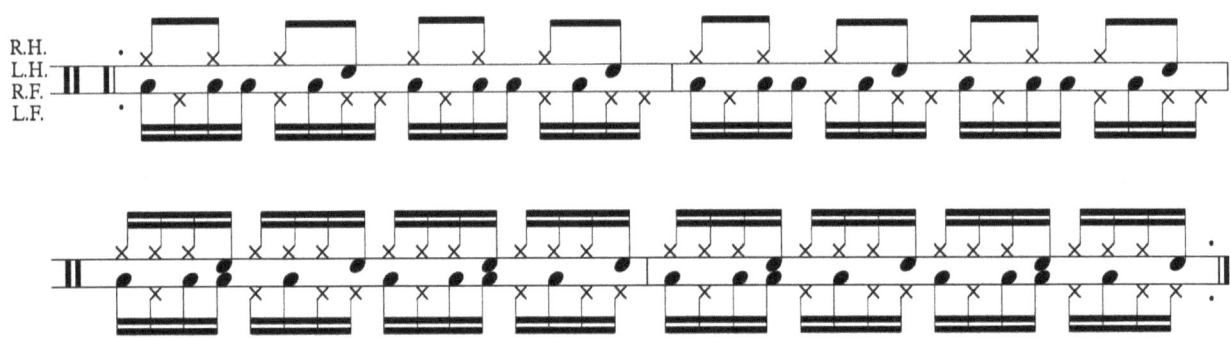

5.a.8.

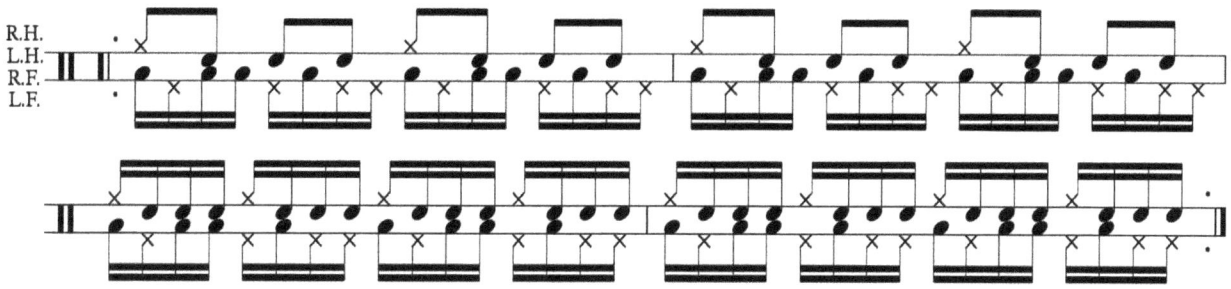

5.a.9.

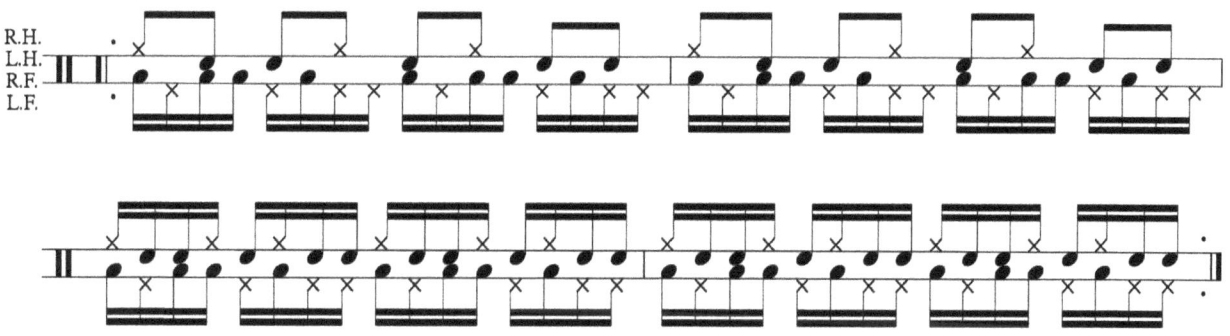

5.a.10.

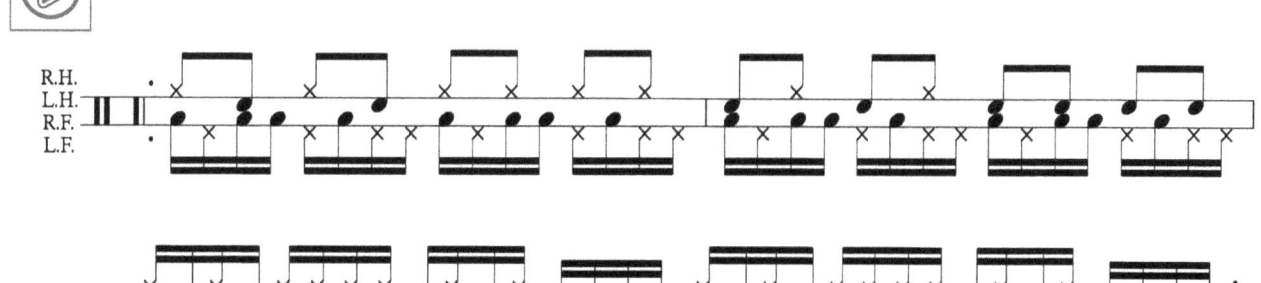

5.a.11.

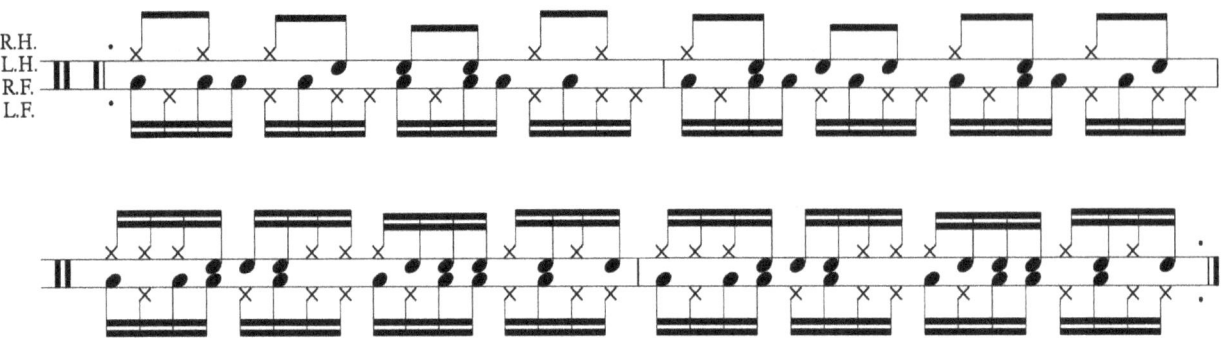

Remember to practice all of the hand variations starting with the opposite hand.

Once you feel comfortable playing the same pattern as both eighth notes and sixteenth notes with the two limbs that are not playing the ostinato, it is time to start combining the patterns.

5.B.- Concept Development Part 2 - Changing Patterns Over an Ostinato

In order to improvise over an ostinato, we need to be able to play different patterns over the ostinato, not just the same pattern with different note values. In this section, we maintain the paradiddle ostinato with the feet as sixteenth notes, but change the patterns played with the hands without changing the subdivision. Each pattern is played for two bars before switching and starts with four bars per example.

5.b.1.

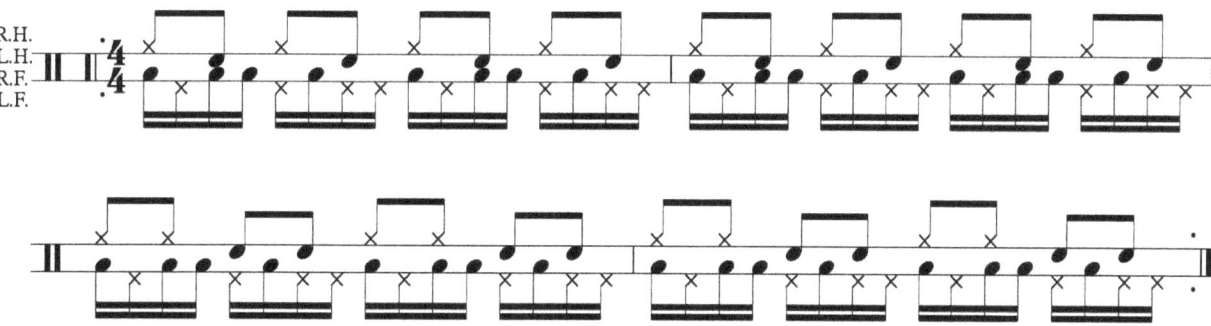

5.b.2.

5.b.3.

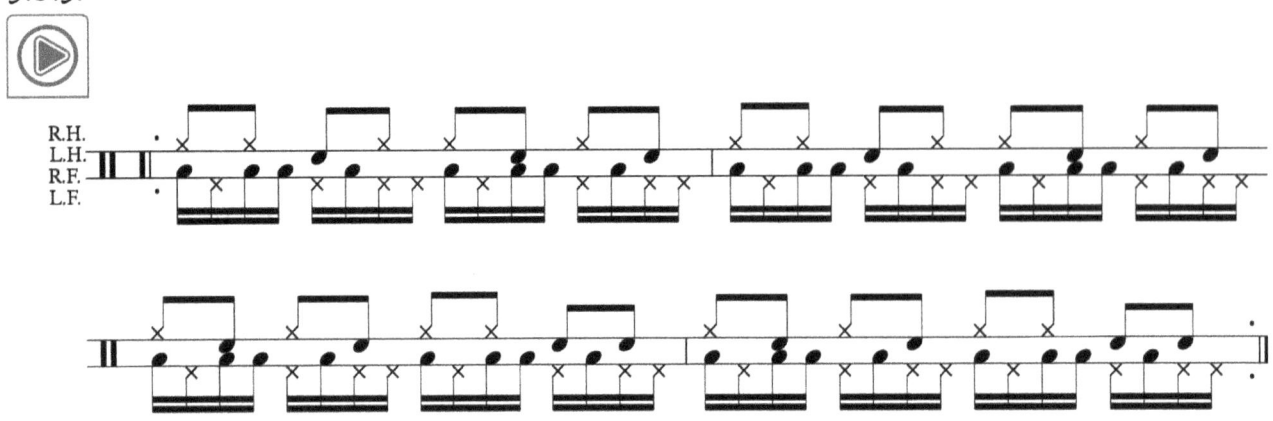

5.b.4.

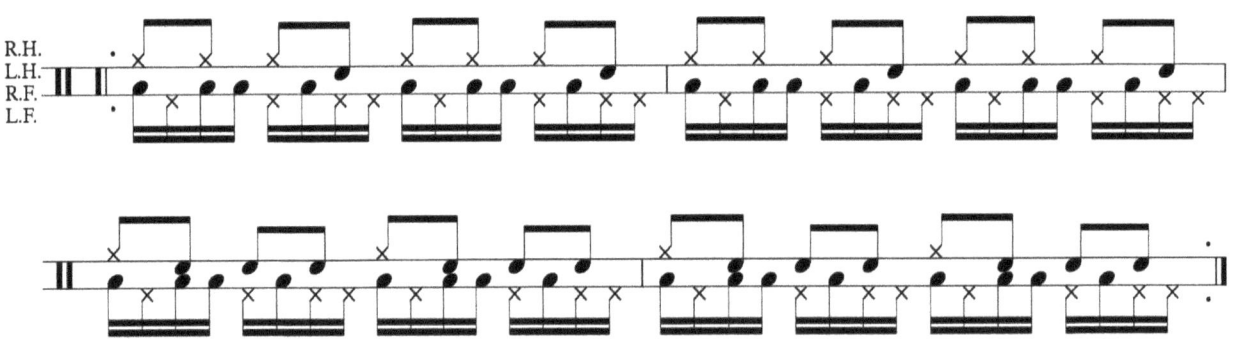

5.b.5.

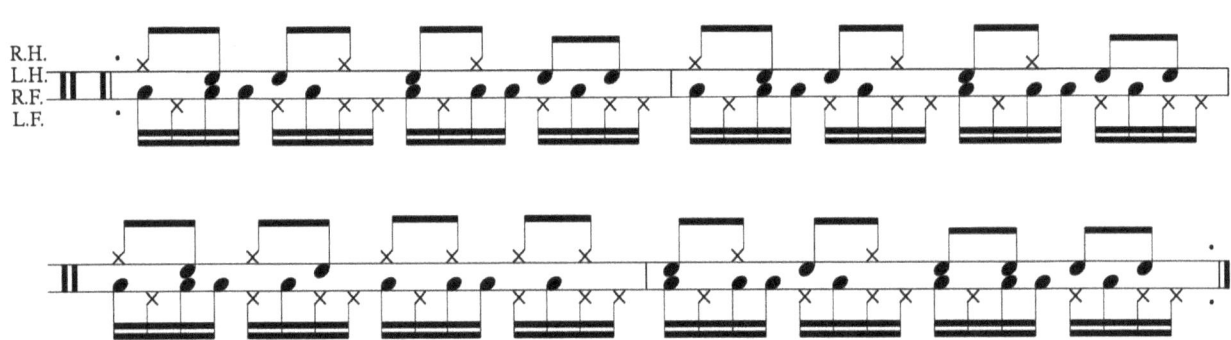

5.b.6.

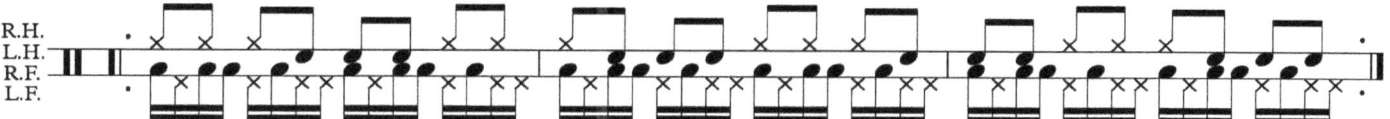

You may have noticed that the hand patterns written in the first section of this chapter were repeated. Using familiar patterns might help you to feel more comfortable with the transitions. Once again, I encourage you to write your own patterns in order to express your own voice, especially when working on improvisation.

5.b.7.

The next example is all of the hand patterns studied in section 5.A. together written as a 22-bar phrase over the paradiddle ostinato with the feet.

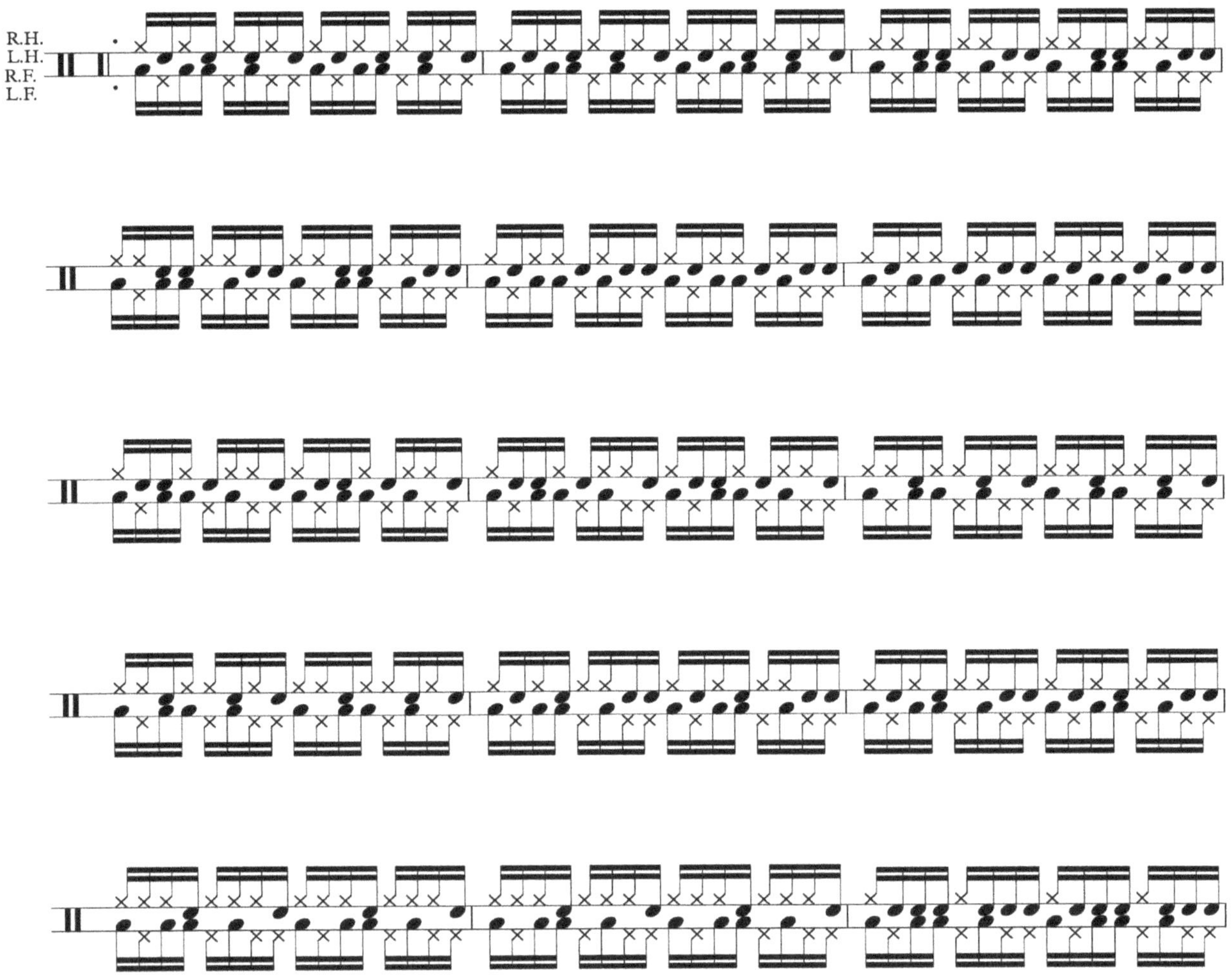

The previous example is the longest exercise in this book up until this point. In addition to further developing your skill set, its purpose is to inspire you to create your own patterns to expand your creativity behind the kit.

Remember that all of the patterns previously written in this book can be used as ostinatos and/or patterns and that you can change the set of limbs that play the ostinato. For example, you could play the paradiddle between your left foot and left hand instead of playing it with your feet.

5.C.- Concept Development Part 3 - Groove Development Over an Ostinato

After exploring two-limb ostinato ideas, we explore single-limb ostinatos. You may be wondering why the single-limb ostinato is being practiced after the two-limb ostinato and the answer is simple: *the more free limbs we have, the harder it is to improvise.* Sustaining an ostinato with two limbs means we are only free to improvise with the other two limbs, which is not necessarily too difficult. However, having three limbs free to improvise makes the task much more challenging.

This section presents two different ostinatos with the left foot while playing grooves with the rest of the limbs. The left foot ostinatos are groups of three sixteenth notes, or a dotted eight note, and groups of five sixteenth notes. The grooves will be based on the bass drum and the snare always playing one note, which will change in duration by one sixteenth note in order to explore all of the placement possibilities.

5.c.1.

The first groove is the bass drum on beat one and the snare on beat three, which separates them by eight sixteenth notes. The left foot is a dotted eighth note, or three sixteenth notes, and the right hand plays a rhythmic figure of one eighth note and two sixteenth notes. In order for the grouping of three and the groove to restart on beat one, it is written as a three-bar phrase.

Note that the notation has changed to standard drum notation!

5.c.2.

The next step is to play the bass drum and the snare every seven sixteenth notes while maintaining the same rhythmic pattern with the right hand and the groups of three with the left foot. In order for this example to restart on beat one, it requires two bars of 21/8. If we were to keep this example in 4/4, it would require 21 bars before it would restart on beat one. For the sake of simplicity, think of this next example in 21/8.

Note that the rhythmic figure played with the right hand "flips" in the second bar due to the time signature.

5.c.3.

The next step is to play the bass drum and the snare every six sixteenth notes while maintaining the same rhythmic patterns with the right hand and the left foot. In order for this example to restart on beat one, it requires three bars of 4/4.

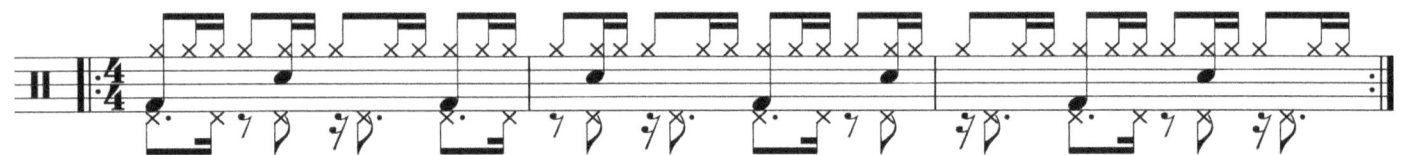

5.c.4.

Now we play the bass drum and the snare every five sixteenth notes. The time signature is 5/4 and it requires three bars for the dotted eighth note and the groove to restart on beat one.

5.c.5.

The next step is to play the bass drum and the snare every four sixteenth notes, which creates a typical two and four groove. This results in a three-bar phrase in 4/4.

5.c.6.

Now we play the bass drum and the snare every three sixteenth notes. Notice that this groove aligns with the left foot ostinato. Remember to count so that you don't lose the original pulse. This example requires one bar in 3/4.

5.c.7.

The last possibility is to play the bass drum and the snare every two sixteenth notes. This example results in one bar of 3/4.

5.c.8.

In order to improvise over the dotted eighth note ostinato with the left foot, we need to be able to transition between all of the different groupings played with the bass drum and the snare. This next example is a combination of all of the previous variations. It starts with the bass drum and the snare playing every eight sixteenth notes for two bars, then every seven, then every six, and so on. After that, it then reverses the exercise by the bass drum and the snare playing every three sixteenth notes, then every four, and so on, until it returns to every eight sixteenth notes.

To simplify the reading, the entire example is written in 4/4. This helps to practice improvising in 4/4 over the dotted eighth note pattern with the left foot, which is a more likely scenario in a musical setting. Remember to count throughout the entire example to ensure that you know where beat one is, *always*.

ADVANCED DRUMMING COORDINATION

Remember that this ostinato can be played with any limb. Explore all of the possibilities to achieve a better understanding of improvisation using groups of three.

5.c.9.

Now we repeat the same process to explore groups of five with the left foot.

5.c.10.

5.c.11.

5.c.12.

5.c.13.

5.c.14.

5.c.15.

5.c.16.

5.D.- Concept Development Part 4 - Layered Ostinatos

Once playing ostinatos with one or two limbs feels comfortable, it is time to introduce layered ostinatos. Playing unisons is one of the most difficult tasks behind the kit. Therefore, playing ostinatos that include unisons creates a considerable technical challenge.

This section applies the different steps presented in the previous chapters to break down one layered ostinato. Keep in mind that these are the recommended steps to follow for any ostinato, but not all of the possibilities.

5.d.1.

Introducing the ostinato:

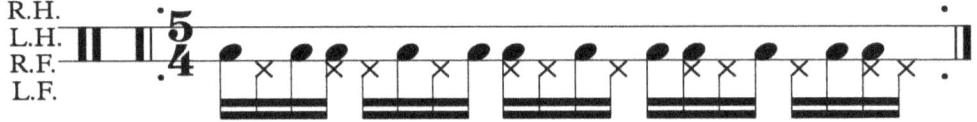

5.d.2.

Choose a pattern to play over it – in this case, the single stroke roll – and play it as eighth notes over the ostinato.

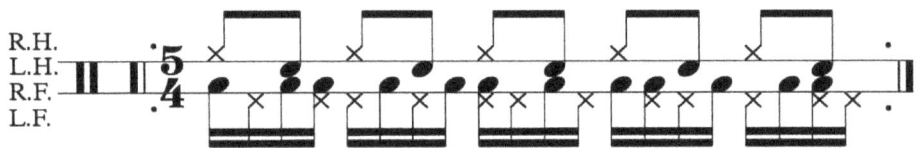

5.d.3.

Now, play the same pattern, the single stroke roll, as sixteenth notes over the ostinato.

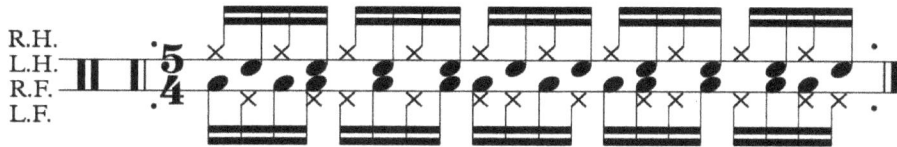

5.d.4.

The next set of examples combines eighth notes and sixteenth notes over the ostinato in different grooves.

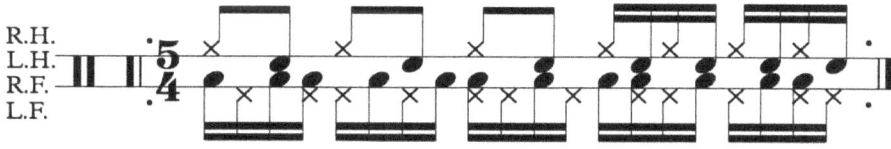

5.d.5.

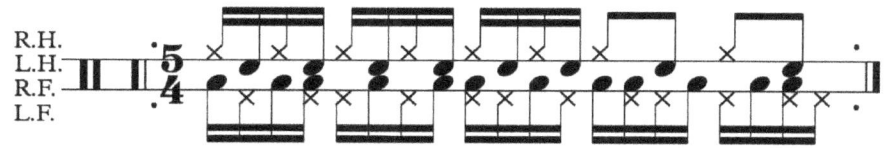

5.d.6.

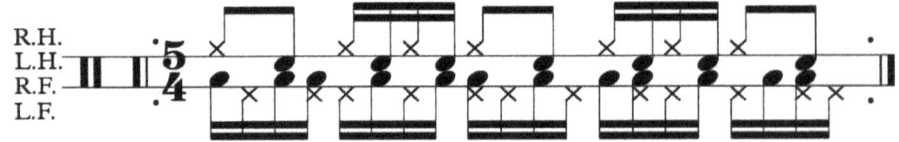

5.d.7.

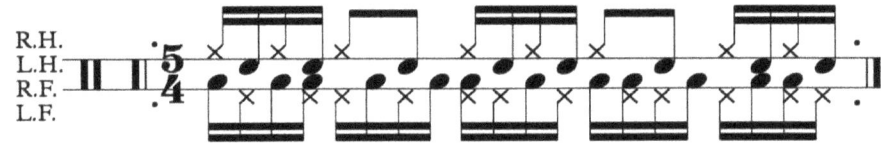

5.d.8.

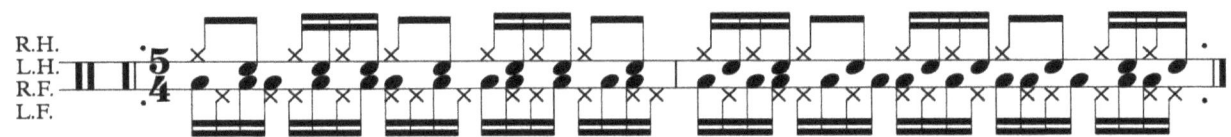

5.d.9.

The next set of examples integrates different rhythmic ideas with different patterns over the same ostinato.

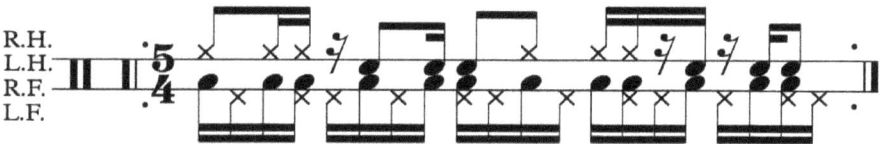

5.d.10.

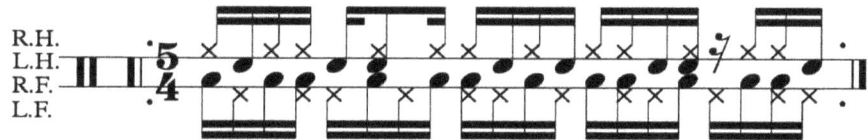

5.d.11.

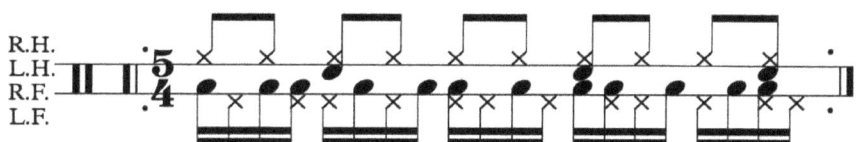

5.d.12.

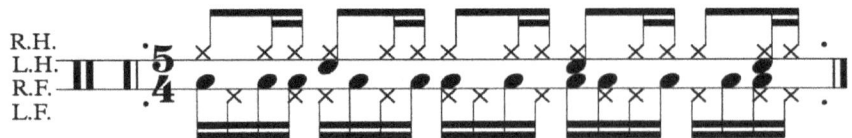

5.d.13.
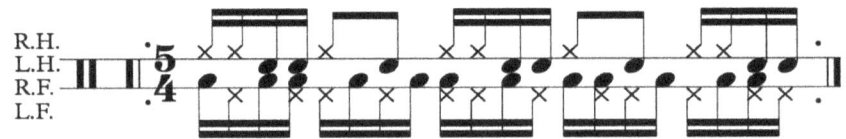

5.d.14.

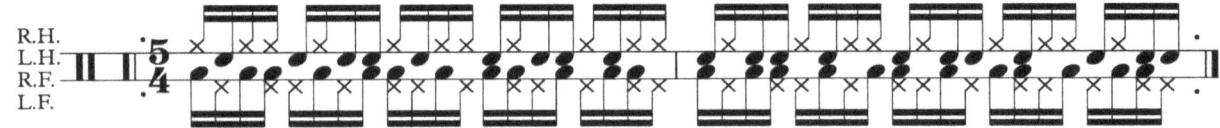

ADVANCED DRUMMING COORDINATION

The next examples are a few more ideas of layered ostinatos to explore. Note that there are no specific limbs written for the ostinatos in order to give you creative freedom. There are also no variations or patterns written and it is up to you to exhaust as many possibilities as you can and express your own voice.

5.d.15.

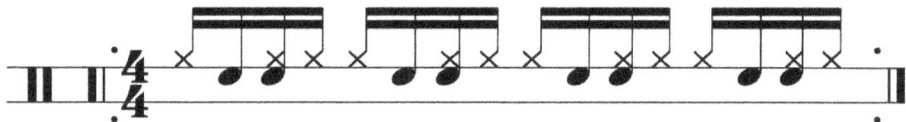

5.d.16.

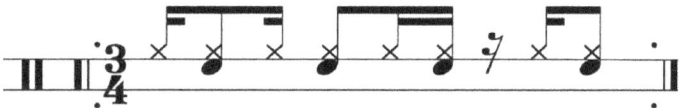

5.d.17.

5.d.18.

5.d.19.

5.d.20.

• CHAPTER 6 •

Using Coordination to Improve Technique

This chapter utilizes coordination exercises to improve technique. Many drummers find it difficult to practice technical exercises for long periods of time. If we combine technical exercises with interesting, but not too challenging, coordination exercises, then practicing technique becomes much more entertaining.

So far, all of the examples in this book were written with one goal in mind: to improve coordination behind the drum set. However, there is a direct correlation between technique and coordination. For example, you may have found a need to improve a specific area of your technique to help you play some of the coordination examples in this book. This is because our ability to gain coordination is often directly related to our ability to proficiently sustain a complex pattern for a long period of time, which requires good technique.

6.A.- Concept Development Part 1 - Accents and Flams Over an Ostinato

The following examples are simple, yet musical, and entertaining ostinato patterns. To improve technique, establish the ostinato and then practice the following series of exercises over it, slowing increasing the tempo.

6.a.1.

Introducing the ostinato:

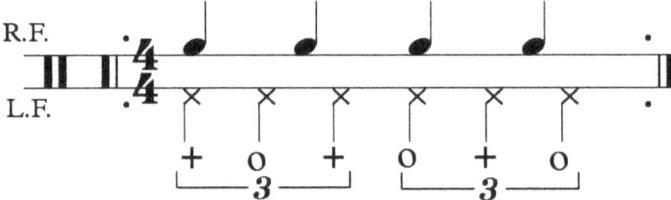

6.a.2.

Below are several common patterns to play over the ostinato.

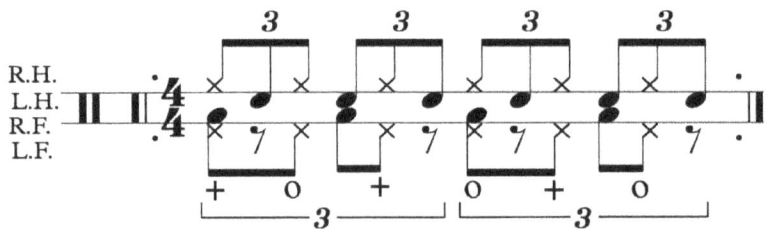

6.a.3.

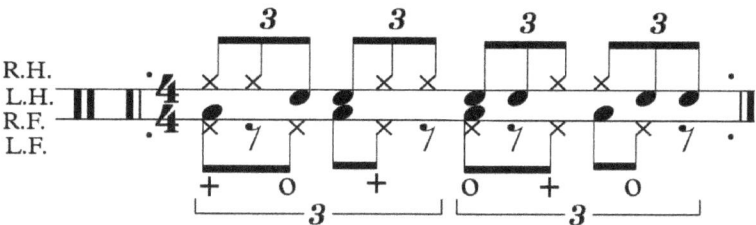

6.a.4.

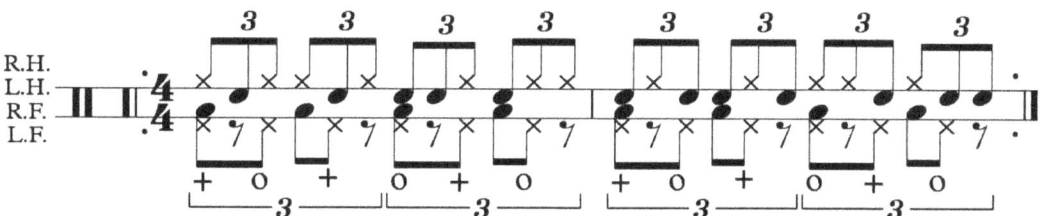

6.a.5.

Now, put the three previous examples together in order to create more efficient technique exercises.

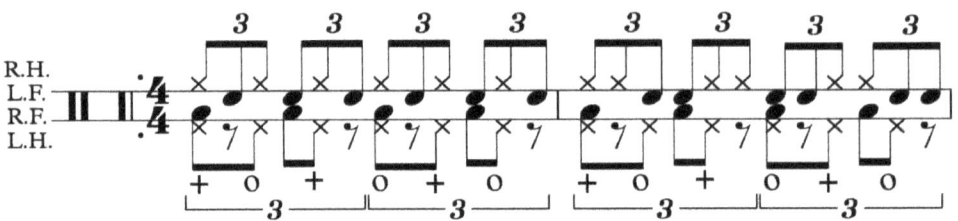

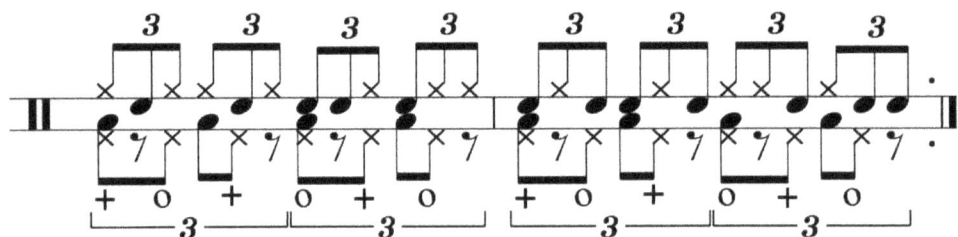

ADVANCED DRUMMING COORDINATION

6.a.6.

Once comfortable with the previous example, it is time to add accents and move around the kit. Pay attention to how the accents emphasize the polyrhythmic feel of this exercise in particular and remember to always count. *Once again, the notation changes to standard drum notation.*

6.a.7.

6.a.8.

Next, change the hand pattern to work on flams. Play the flam accent over the same ostinato.

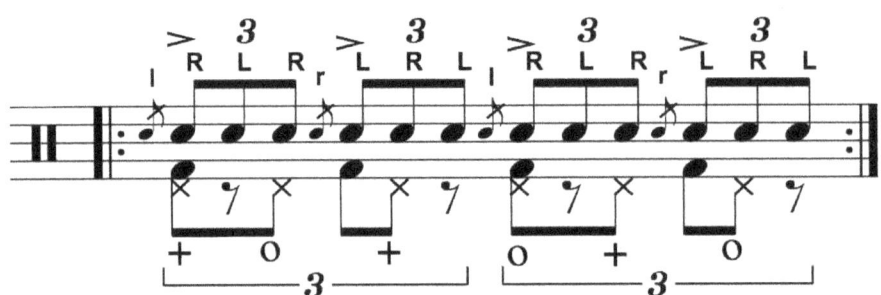

6.a.9.

Now, move the same pattern around the kit.

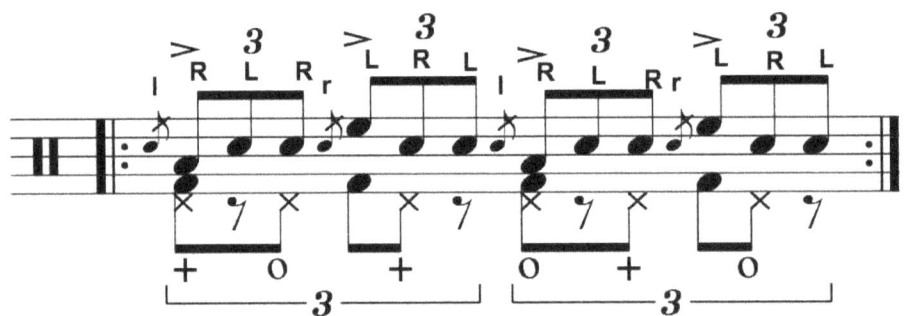

6.a.10.

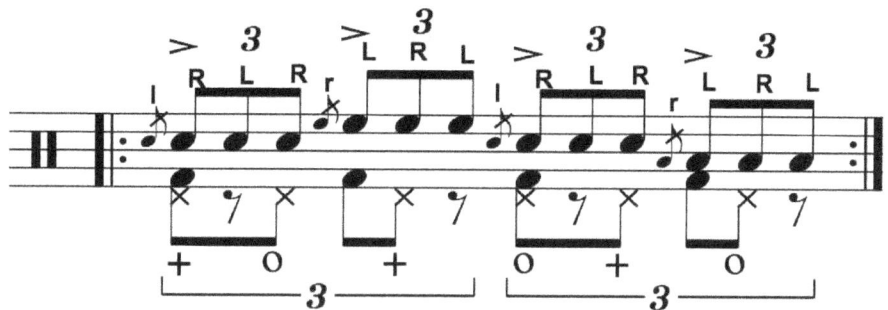

6.a.11.

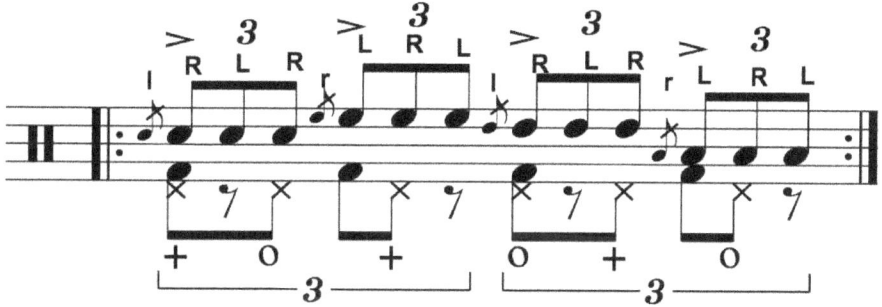

6.a.12.

Remember to use your own ideas over the ostinato. These examples, while common and effective, won't necessarily help you find your own voice behind the kit. Count out loud and practice to a click in order to become comfortable with all of the above variations. Then, begin improvising and expressing yourself.

ADVANCED DRUMMING COORDINATION

6.B.- Concept Development Part 2 - Accents and Diddles Over an Ostinato

This section starts by changing the subdivision to sixteenth notes. The ostinato used in the next set of examples presents an additional technical challenge for the feet and not just the hands. Practicing ostinatos like this one provides a complete workout behind the kit, improving both technique and coordination.

6.b.1.

Introducing the ostinato:

Rhythmically, this ostinato may sound familiar, as it is groups of three played as sixteenth notes with two limbs. However, it requires a little more attention because of what the left foot is playing. This ostinato plays two different voices at the same time with the left foot: the bass drum and the hi-hat. To achieve this, play the bass drum with the left foot using a double pedal and simultaneously step on the hi-hat. This creates a very interesting ostinato sonically because you can hear continuous sixteenth notes with the bass drum, but you can also hear groups of three on the hi-hat.

6.b.2.

In the next set of examples, the hands play the single stroke roll as sixteenth notes. The technical challenge is created by the different accent patterns. Pay attention to the time signatures because they change in order to fit each complete rhythmic phrase into one bar. In this example, the accents create groups of four.

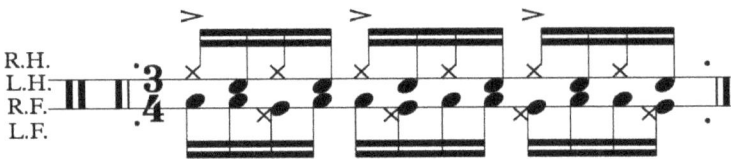

6.b.3.

Now, the accents create groups of three.

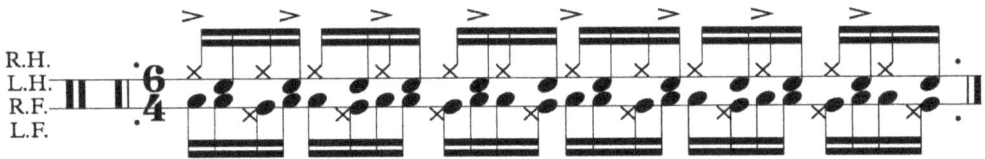

ADVANCED DRUMMING COORDINATION

6.b.4.

The accents in this example create groups of five.

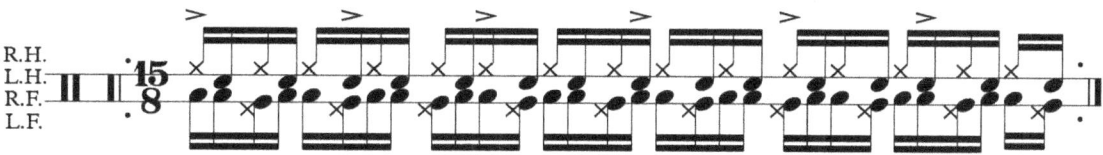

6.b.5.

In the next set of examples, the hands play different patterns. In this example, the hands play the paradiddle over the ostinato, which accentuates every fourth sixteenth note.

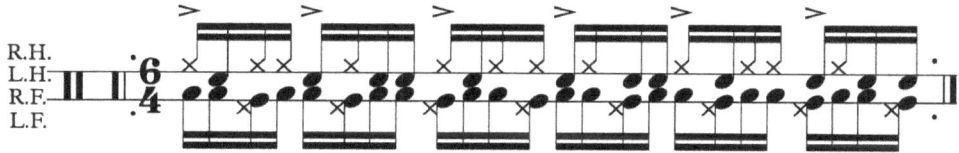

6.b.6.

In this example, the hands play the double paradiddle over the ostinato, which accentuates every sixth sixteenth note.

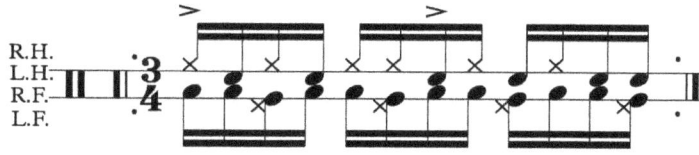

• 111 •

6.b.7.

Next, add diddles to the patterns to continue developing technique and coordination. This makes the examples more challenging because the hands and feet are not always playing in unison even though the underlying subdivision is the same. The first step is to replace the previously accented notes with diddles.

In the first example, the diddles create groups of three.

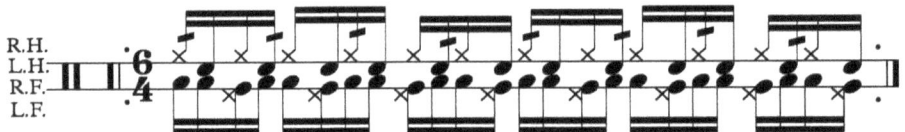

Pay extra attention to the subdivision of the diddles to be sure that it is two thirty-second notes. If this subdivision is not clear, the example will sound out of time.

6.b.8.

In the next example, the diddles create groups of four.

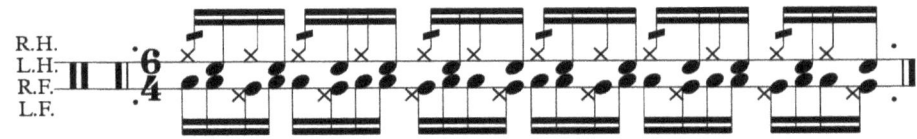

6.b.9.

Now, the diddles create groups of five.

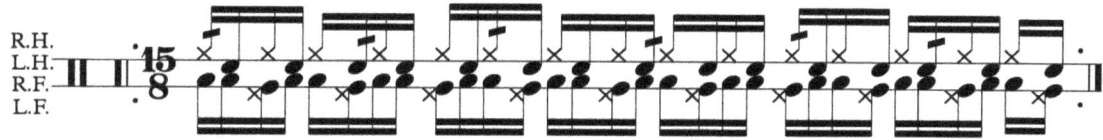

6.b.10.

As in earlier chapters, this next example repeats the previous three variations for two bars each. This creates a more complete workout. Remember to count all the way through the example and pay attention to the time signatures.

ADVANCED DRUMMING COORDINATION

6.b.11.

The next set of examples moves the placement of the diddles to the unaccented notes of the previous patterns. However, the accent patterns remain the same. In this example, the accents create groups of three.

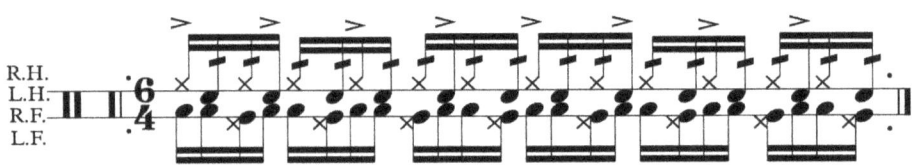

6.b.12.

Now, the accents create groups of four.

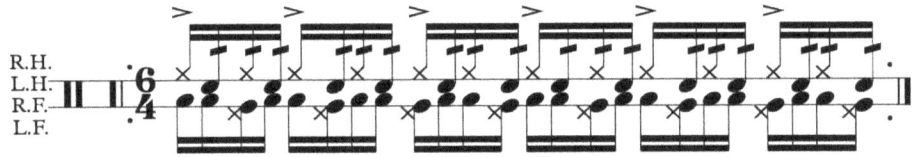

6.b.13.

In this example, the accents create groups of five.

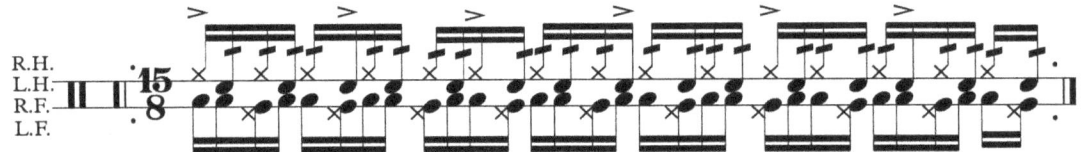

6.b.14.

Once again, this next example repeats the previous three variations for two bars each to create a more complete workout.

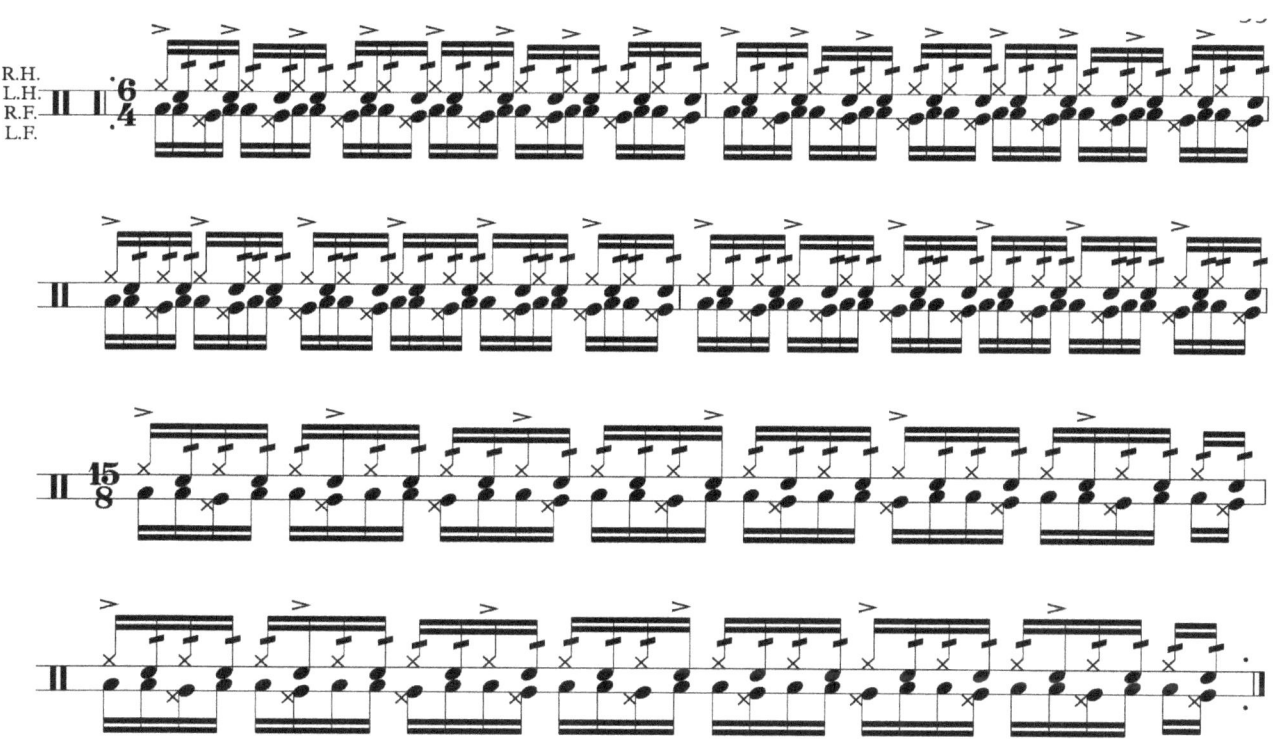

6.b.15.

The next example repeats the previous combination of variations and moves it around the kit. *Note that the notation changes to standard drum notation.*

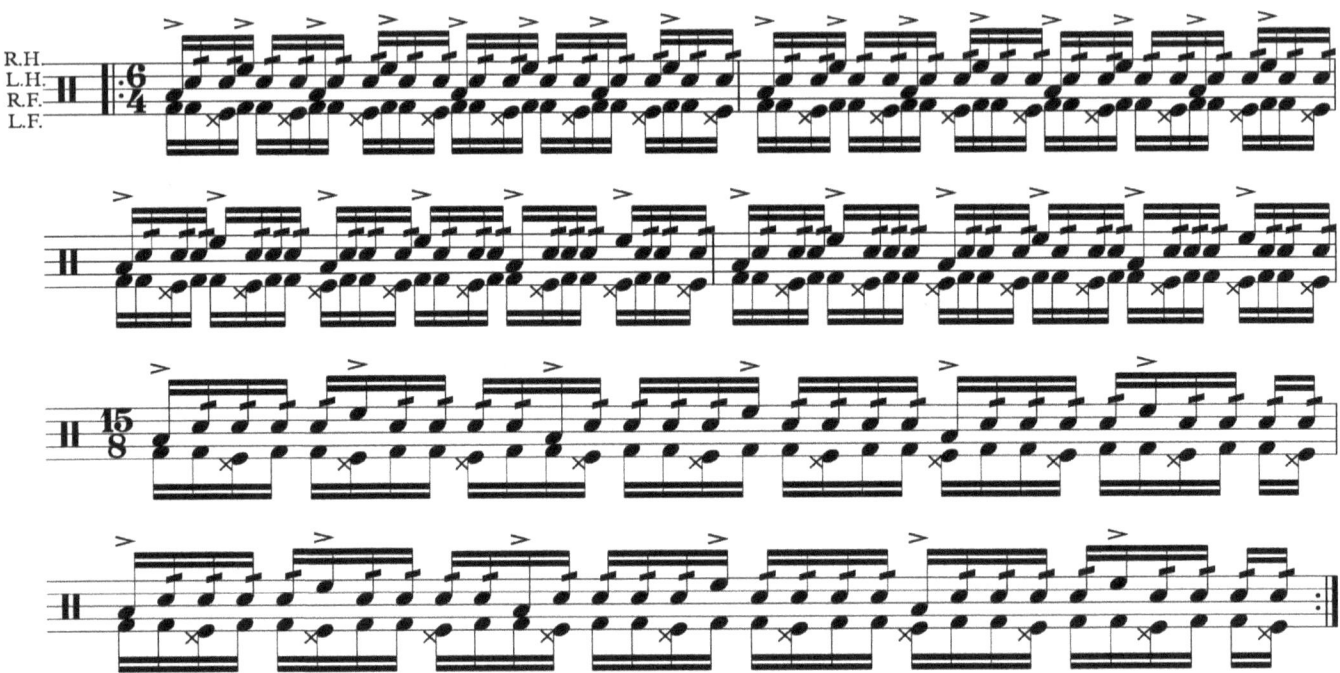

The previous example is written using only one floor tom and one rack tom. If your drum set has more voices than that, feel free to explore them as well. Remember the ultimate goal is to create your own combinations and variations in order to express your own voice.

• CHAPTER 7 •

Nested Tuplets

When people think about complex concepts in music they typically think about complex harmony. By adding extensions to traditional triads, we create more layers and enrich the harmony. A similar level of complexity can be achieved rhythmically by adding layers of rhythm on top of other layers of rhythm.

Nested tuplets are the result of this concept. They are some of the most complicated rhythmic figures we can play, especially when played over other layers of rhythm.

7.A.- Concept Introduction - Single Rhythm Nested Tuplets

Before adding nested tuplets to coordination exercises we first need to understand what nested tuplets are. The simplest explanation is that nested tuplets are the result of subdividing an already existing tuplet, which creates two different tuplets inside of the original pulse. When playing nested tuplets, there are three different layers of rhythm that we must remain aware of:

1. The original pulse
2. The parent tuplet
3. The nested tuplet

For example, when we play a quarter note triplet we subdivide two beats of the original quarter note pulse into three evenly subdivided notes. The quarter note triplet is the parent tuplet in the following set of examples.

7.a.1.

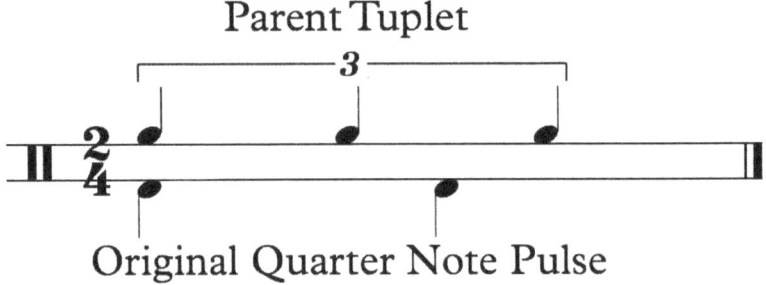

7.a.2.

In this example, subdivide each note of the original parent tuplet into triplets again.

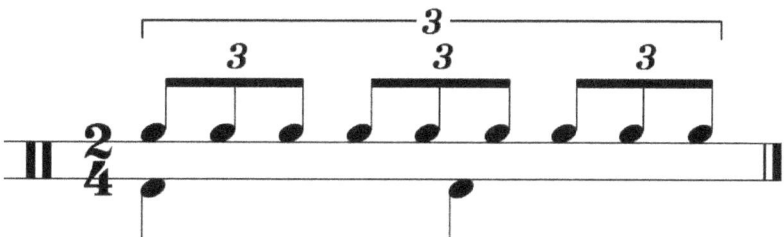

7.a.3.

The previous example could also be written with the polyrhythm created by the parent tuplet notated in the bracket above the new smaller subdivision.

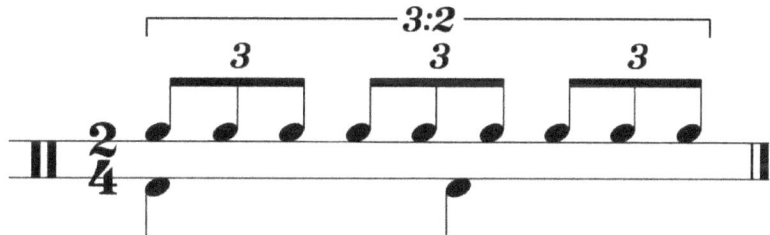

It is important to realize that the previous example is also a polyrhythm of 9:2. However, thinking about it as 9:2 may change which notes are naturally emphasized. Nested tuplets are useful to specify exact phrasing when playing more complex rhythms.

In this chapter, the notation for the parent tuplets follows the notation in example 7.a.2.

7.a.4.

Once you are comfortable playing a rhythmic idea that involves nested tuplets with two limbs, add the rest of the limbs to practice more challenging coordination concepts.

For this example, use the same rhythm written in example 7.a.2. and split the rhythmic idea between all four limbs. The right foot plays the original quarter note pulse, the left foot plays the parent tuplet, and the hands split the nested tuplet.

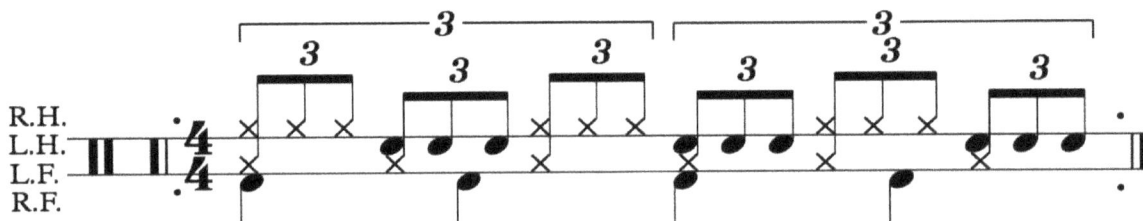

7.a.5.

The next example demonstrates how to break down the previous example to ensure that all of the rhythms are properly subdivided. Practicing methodically allows us to maintain the original pulse and add layers of coordination systematically, which reinforces both the aural and technical comprehension of the nested tuplet. Follow this process to practice all of the subsequent exercises.

7.a.6.

The next step is to change the hand pattern to create more interesting rhythmic phrases. This also creates a more complex coordination challenge.

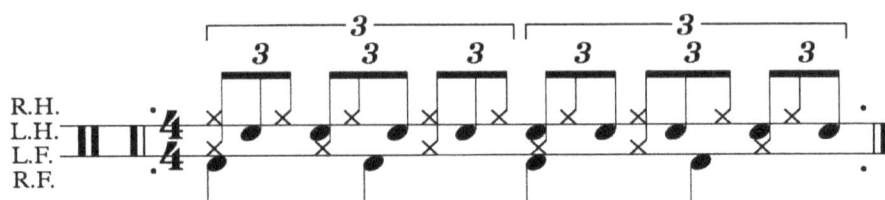

7.a.7.

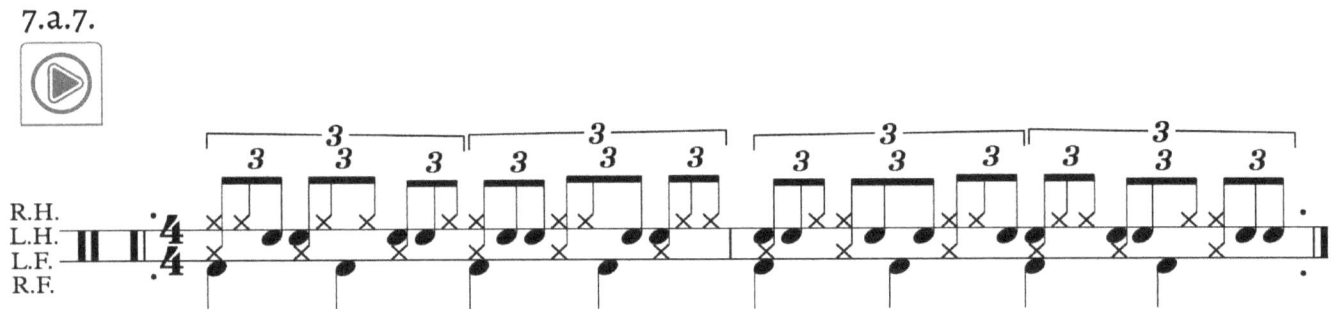

7.a.8.

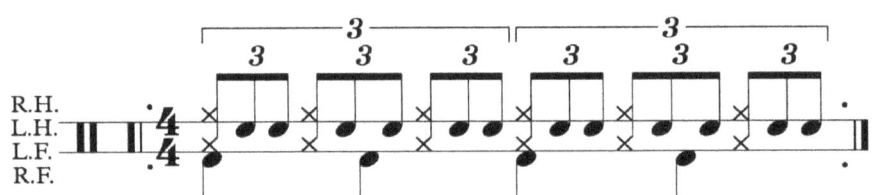

7.a.9.

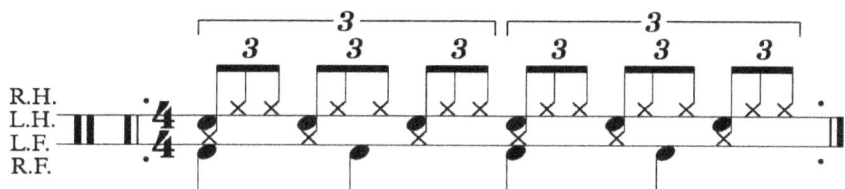

Remember that you can change which limb plays which rhythm. For example, play the quarter note pulse with the left foot and the parent tuplet with the right foot, etc.

7.B.- Concept Development Part 1 - Different Subdivisions of Nested Tuplets

Once you are comfortable playing nested tuplets as one subdivision (in the previous section the nested tuplets were triplets), it is time to change the subdivision. We still use quarter notes for the original pulse and quarter note triplets for the parent tuplet.

7.b.1.

7.b.2.

7.b.3.

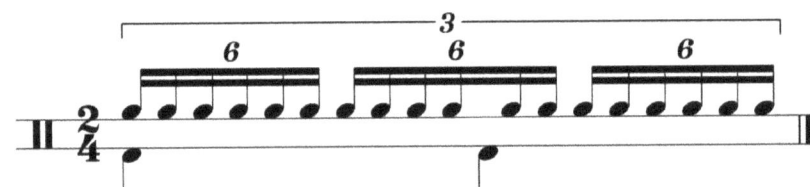

ADVANCED DRUMMING COORDINATION

7.b.4.

Now put the previous examples together to practice the transitions between the different subdivisions of the nested tuplets. Play the example in 4/4.

7.b.5.

The next set of examples includes different patterns that can be used to practice four-way coordination while integrating the various nested tuplet subdivisions presented above.

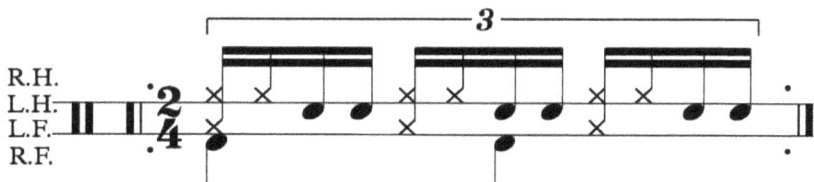

7.b.6.

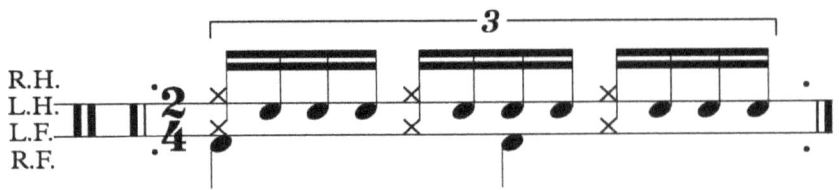

7.b.7.

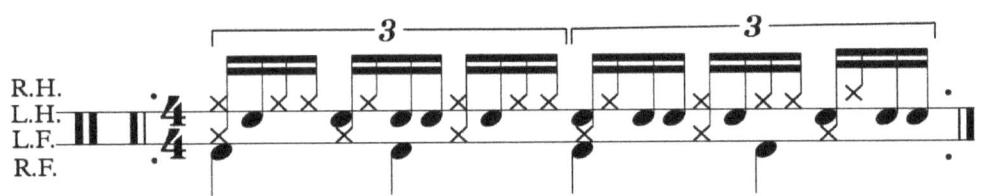

7.b.8.

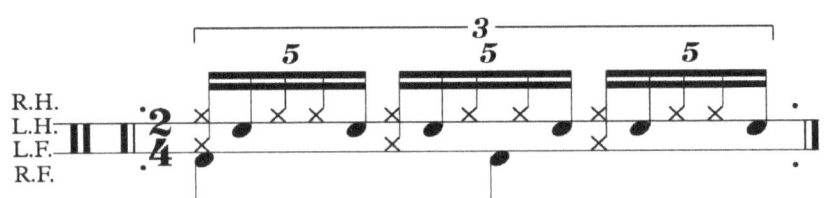

7.b.9.

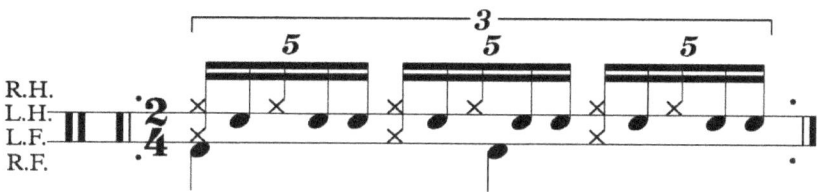

7.b.10.

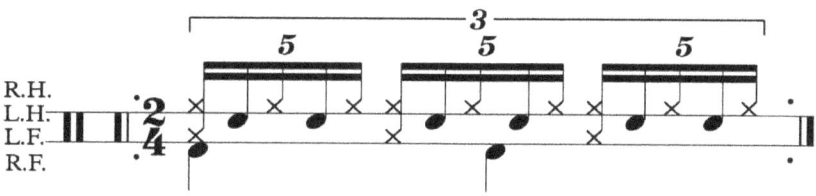

7.b.11.

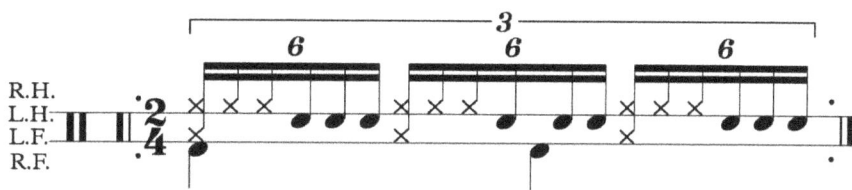

RAY ROJO

7.b.12.

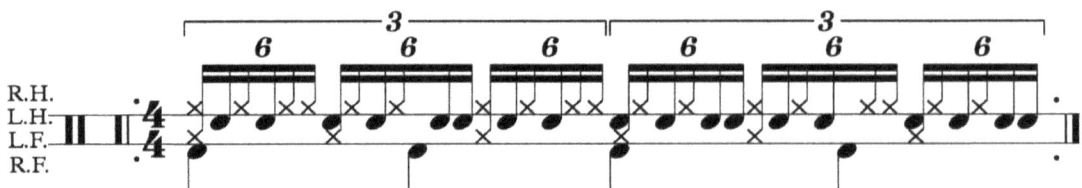

7.C.- Concept Development Part 2 - Rhythmic Combinations of Nested Tuplets

After studying and practicing several nested tuplet subdivisions, we need to study and pratice the different subdivisions together. This is an incredibly challenging rhythmic concept. The ability to switch back and forth between different nested tuplet subdivisions while sustaining the original pulse is the ultimate goal to successfully integrate nested tuplets into improvisation.

In the following examples, notice that the nested tuplets are all written as one voice and there is no suggested hand written to the left of the staff. I encourage you to find the stickings that are the most comfortable for each individual example by combining single and double strokes in order to not lose your place in the bar.

7.c.1.

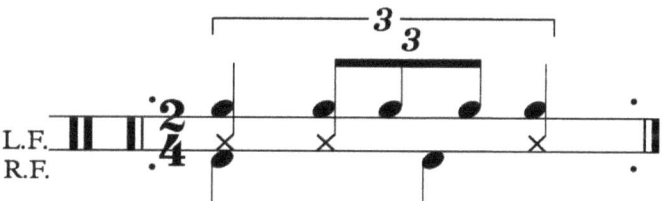

7.c.2.

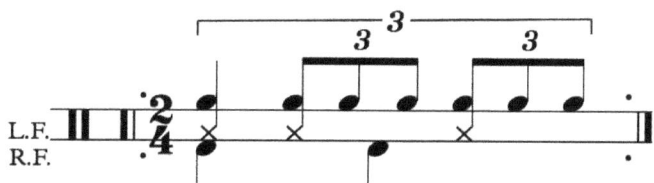

7.c.3.

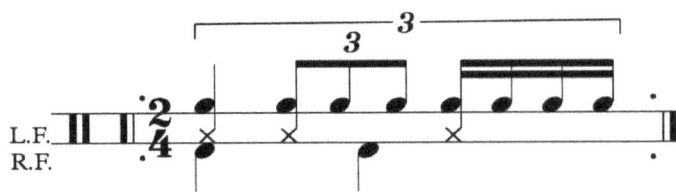

7.c.4.

7.c.5.

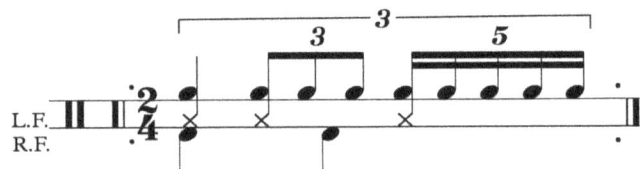

7.c.6.

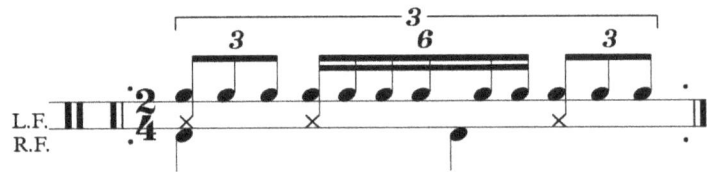

ADVANCED DRUMMING COORDINATION

7.D.- Suggested Nested Tuplets

All of the nested tuplets in this chapter have used a polyrhythm of 3:2 (or the quarter note triplet as the parent tuplet). However, the same concept can be applied to any other polyrhythm. This chapter concludes with several examples of nested tuplets that utilize different parent tuplets. Remember all of the steps that we followed in the first three sections of this chapter. Apply them to the following examples to explore the endless rhythmic possibilities in the world of nested tuplets.

7.d.1.

Start with the polyrhythm of 4:3 as the parent tuplet.

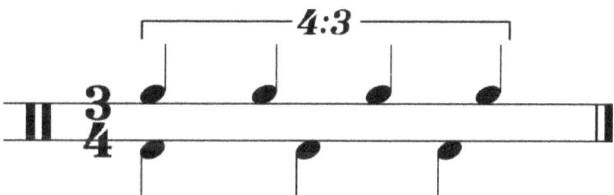

7.d.2.

This example subdivides the parent tuplet into sixteenth notes.

7.d.3.

Now, practice the polyrhythm of 5:2 as the parent tuplet.

7.d.4.

This example subdivides the parent tuplet into triplets.

7.d.5.

Next, practice the polyrhythm of 5:4 as the parent tuplet.

ADVANCED DRUMMING COORDINATION

7.d.6.

This example subdivides the parent tuplet into sixteenth notes.

7.d.7.

Now, practice the polyrhythm of 5:3 as the parent tuplet.

7.d.8.

This example subdivides the parent tuplet into triplets.

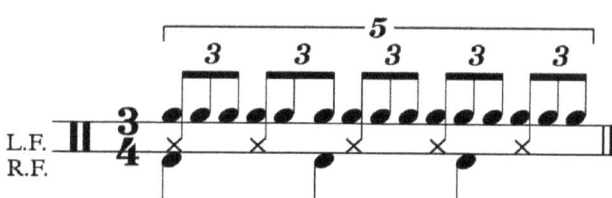

Remember that any of the combinations used in the earlier chapters of this book may also be applied to nested tuplet ideas. None of the examples in this book are limited to the way they are written and again I encourage you to exhaust all of the possibilities you can find and create.

• CHAPTER 8 •

Musical Examples and Transcriptions

One of the most common questions I hear when discussing subjects like the ones in this book is, "Why should I spend years practicing something that I am never going to play?" The answer is simple. Anything you practice that pushes you beyond your comfort zone will result in improvement. In addition, if you *can* play it, then you *will* use it. It is a lack of experience that prevents us from playing more complex rhythmic ideas in musical contexts, *not* the lack of musicality in the ideas themselves.

There are abundant examples of drummers playing extremely advanced coordination concepts in music. The more you familiarize yourself with these ideas, the more frequently you will recognize them. In this chapter, I break down two pieces I composed that apply similar concepts to the ones discussed in this book.

8.A.- Transcription and Analysis and of "Over the Trees"

I composed "Over the Trees" in 2013. Rhythmically, it is based on a three-note ostinato played between the left foot and the left hand; however, it becomes a six-note ostinato because the left hand changes surfaces. This idea shows up twice in the piece, first in the introduction and then again in the bridge.

The time signature in the introduction changes based on the groove played between the right hand and the right foot. It is not based on the ostinato. The bottom staff represents the left foot, which plays the hi-hat, and the left hand, which switches back and forth between an auxiliary snare and the hi-hat. The top staff represents the right foot, which always plays the bass drum and is written on the lowest space of the staff, and the right hand, which switches back and forth between the main snare drum and the floor tom.

Here is a transcription of the introduction of the piece:

8.a.1.

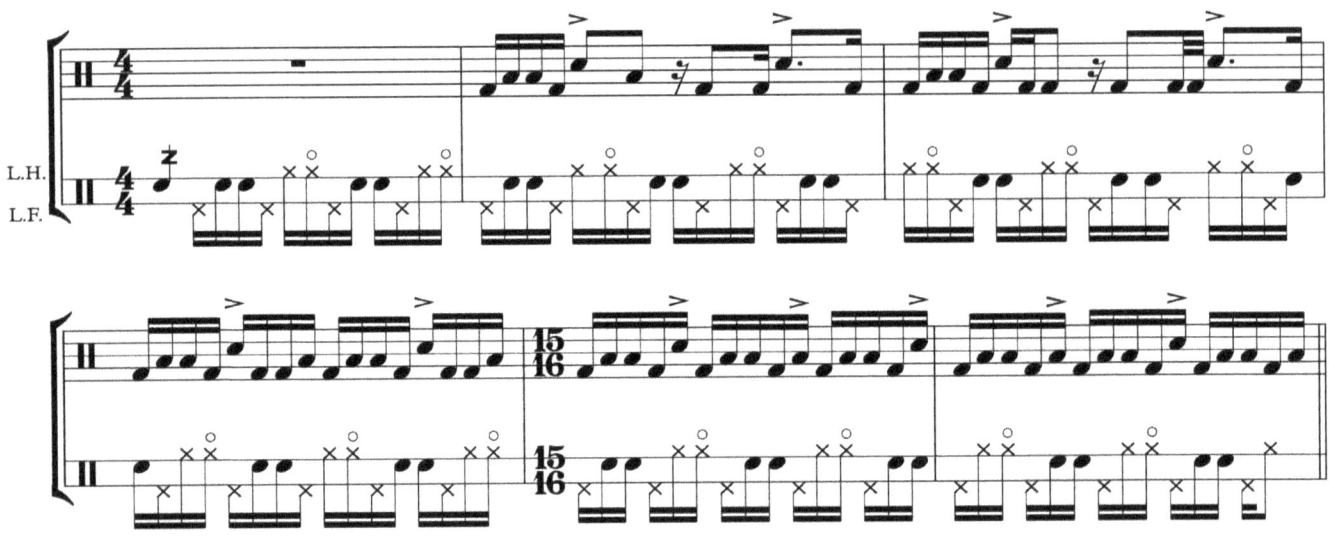

"Over the Trees" introduces the ostinato in the first bar and the groove in the second bar. It may be interesting to know that I wrote the groove first and added the ostinato later.

8.a.2.

Let's analyze the ostinato from "Over the Trees".

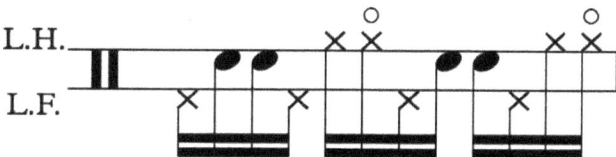

You may have noticed that there is no time signature attached to the ostinato in this example. Because the time signature changes frequently in the piece, thinking of the ostinato in this way allows us to focus more on the groove instead of the ostinato itself. Remember that the left hand switches surfaces. It starts on the auxiliary snare and then moves to the hi-hat. Playing the hi-hat with the left hand while opening it with the left foot creates an interesting sound and can lead the listener into thinking there are extra voices.

Allow yourself plenty of time to feel comfortable playing the ostinato on its own before you add the groove over it. Pay extra attention to the left hand playing the hi-hat to ensure that the sound of the open hi-hat only occurs on the sixth note of the pattern.

8.a.3.

Once you are comfortable with the ostinato, analyze the groove played by the right foot and the right hand. The first two bars of the groove are loosely based on the sound of the inverted paradiddle and are used to set up the third bar.

8.a.4.

The third bar plays the complete inverted paradiddle between the bass drum and the right hand.

The time signature is 4/4 because it is an inverted paradiddle.

8.a.5.

In the last two bars of the introduction, the time signature changes to 15/16 because of the groove played by the right hand and the right foot. The groove in these two bars changes to groups of five with a backbeat on the snare on the last note of every other group of five.

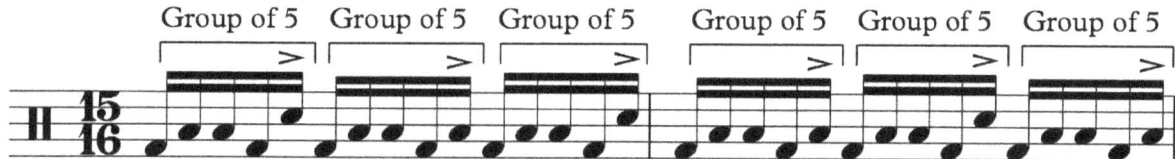

It is essential to realize that the bracket of five is there to help you recognize the artificial groupings of five sixteenth notes and does *not* represent quintuplets. The two bars of 15/16 are used to set up the "A" section of the piece, which is also in 15/16.

8.a.6.

The next section of "Over the Trees" that we analyze is the bridge. I include the full score in order to demonstrate how the drum part relates to the rest of the instruments.

The bridge begins very similarly to the introduction of the piece by setting up the ostinato first. What is interesting about the bridge is how the rest of the parts relate to the drum part. Throughout the bridge, the bass plays a dotted eighth note rhythm, which lines up with the left foot hi-hat. This means that the bass accentuates the dotted eighth note in the ostinato. The guitar and the keyboard play the same melody and rhythm as the drums in the first bar of the bridge. Then, the keyboard plays in unison with the drums while the guitar accentuates the groups of five with a different rhythm.

This is an example of how advanced rhythmic patterns behind the drum set can be used to bring the sound of the band together into one cohesive and musical unit.

8.B.- Transcription and Analysis of "Travieso"

I composed "Travieso" in 2017. This piece also has a section with an ostinato between the left hand and the left foot. In this piece, the ostinato is part of the groove that accompanies the bass solo. The purpose of the ostinato is to use a more intricate rhythm to enhance the simple groove.

Here is a transcription of the drum part during the bass solo:

8.b.1.

The groove played during the bass solo was the first part I wrote for this piece. I was inspired by the ostinato and decided to compose around it.

8.b.2.

Let's analyze the ostinato from "Travieso".

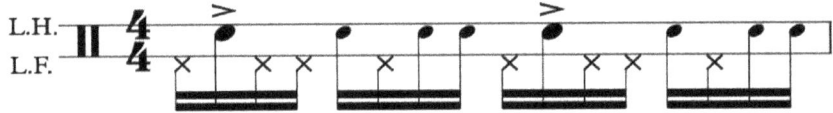

The ostinato is the single paradiddle between the left foot and the left hand. However, the accent is on the second note of the pattern instead of the downbeats. Allow yourself plenty of time to feel comfortable playing the ostinato on its own before you add the groove over it.

8.b.3.

The main groove played over the ostinato is a simple bass drum pattern played with the right foot, primarily eighth notes on an auxiliary hi-hat, and a strong backbeat on the main snare drum on beats two and four. Both the auxiliary hi-hat and the main snare are played with the right hand.

The sound of this groove faintly resembles the sound of the paradiddle. This similarity is what inspired me to play the paradiddle ostinato over it.

8.b.4.

There are some extra hi-hat notes played over the groove in the transcription. The extra hi-hat notes were the result of practicing the following pattern:

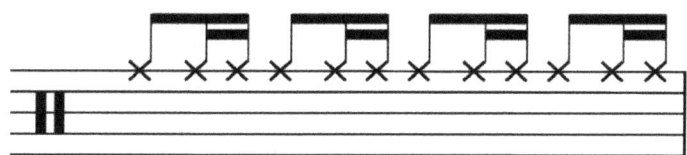

8.b.5.

Here is the full groove with the new hi-hat pattern:

Because playing the entire groove with the extra sixteenth notes sounded too busy and a little distracting, I decided to use a combination of both eighth notes and sixteenth notes in the final recording. I believe that improvising a few extra hi-hats added a nice texture during the bass solo.

Conclusion

Thank you for joining me in the never-ending journey to gain freedom behind the kit. I hope that this comprehensive guide has helped you to develop an advanced level of coordination. Continue to push the limits of your own playing, explore the endless rhythmic possibilities with all four limbs, and develop your own voice behind the instrument. In time, pushing your own limits will result in a level of understanding and ability that will allow you to integrate more advanced rhythmic concepts into the musical settings in which you play.

ABOUT THE AUTHOR

Ray Rojo started playing drums when he was 13 years old. He studied for several years in his hometown, Cuernavaca, Mexico, and then for a short time in Mexico City before moving to Hollywood to attend Musicians Institute (M.I.). At M.I. he earned a Bachelor of Music degree in Performance of Contemporary Styles.

Since moving to Los Angeles, Ray has played and recorded for guitar player Nili Brosh and toured nationally and internationally with guitar players Felix Martin and Lee McKinney. He also recorded drums on the audio examples for the book "Advanced Rhythmic Concepts for Guitar" by Jan Rivera.

As an educator, Ray has taught at Cornel School of Contemporary Music, at Modern Music School, and as a private tutor at M.I. Ray also wrote a six-book beginner drum series entitled "Beginner Series: Drums Method". In addition, Ray records and teaches privately out of his home studio, and is the owner of rayrojodrums.com.

www.ingramcontent.com/pod-product-compliance
Lightning Source LLC
Chambersburg PA
CBHW080342170426
43194CB00014B/2657